BEFORE THERE WERE BARS

AN ANTHOLOGY OF
STORIES, POEMS AND ART

POPS
THE CLUB

Before There Were Bars
An Anthology of Stories, Poems and Art
Copyright © 2016 POPStheclub.com, Inc.

Editors: Amy Friedman and
Dennis Danziger & Alison Longman
Proofreader: Christina Larsen
Book Design by TLC Graphics, *www.TLCGraphics.com*
Cover Design: Tamara Dever; Interior Design: Monica Thomas

Illustrated Portraits © 2016 Doris Longman,
© 2016 Chris Wright
Cover Photograph © 2016 Katherine Secaida
Interior Photographs © 2016 Katherine Secaida,
Juanito Hernandez
POPS the Club logo by Kenny Barela

ISBN 978-0-692-71348-8 (paperback)
ISBN 978-0-692-71371-6 (ebook)

Visit our website www.POPStheclub.com

Table of Contents

BROTHERS & SISTERS — 129

PEOPLE WE LOVE — 143

HOW WE LIVE — 159

WHO WE ARE — 219

NOT THE ONLY ONE — 245

WE THE BRAVE — 259

LOOKING FORWARD, LOOKING BACK — 279

Introduction

Early one February morning I was talking with my friend Anna-Majia about ACES, Adverse Childhood Effects. We agreed: Too many schools favor punishment over praise and school suspension over compassion. Too many of society's young people are lost from the start because of a sometimes heartless system and because of labeling.

Anna-Majia said it succinctly: "In truth it's often the kids who have all the strikes against them who prove to us their resilience. Given one little hand up, one word of praise, they overcome the most daunting odds."

That is some of what I have learned in the three years since we first launched POPS the Club, and after Anna-Majia and I hung up, I walked to the POPS weekly meeting at Venice High with that thought in mind. When I walked in I was struck first by the visceral—the delicious smell of the Factors Famous Deli's cheese casserole, the warm rolls from Manhattan Bread and Bagel and Le Pain Quotidien. Next came one of the kid's Cheetos breath and someone's too-sweet perfume mixed with chalk and salty ocean air and sweat. As always, too, there was the riot of sound: The buzz of broken loudspeakers, clanging bells, fingernails clicking on cell phones; and the sights: grimy linoleum, hoodies and miniskirts, baseball caps and heavy eyeliner, nail polish and red lipstick.

High school classrooms are not beautiful, but every POPS the Club meeting turns those rooms into oases, and I am often brought to my knees in awe of the way those rooms are transformed by kindness, the sound of the voices of the sponsors and volunteers and students cajoling and inspiring and guiding and offering friendship and sometimes solace.

That particular Wednesday a tidal wave of kids poured into the classroom and with them came a sea of volunteers. Dennis, the sponsor, decided to break us into small groups that day for "small group sharing day." He assigned a volunteer to each group. He turned to me and said, "You go there."

Most of the groups were composed of four or five or more students, but Dennis pointed to Yesenia and Jessica who sat alone, a group of their own.

I joined them and Jessica convinced Yesenia to read me her story, *Motherless Girl*. I'd always noticed Yesenia's voice was little girl-like, but as she read, her voice grew stronger and deeper. I learned that when she was 8, she lived with her 28-year-old schizophrenic mother and was "a mother to her mother." When her mom was diagnosed and sent away, child services sent Yesenia to a foster home, then another and another. Finally at 10 she was back with her mom, but when Mom went away again, she returned to foster care. Now, at 16—just 16—she is back with her mom, being a mother again. "We need each other," Yesenia said. Jessica put her hand on her friend's hand.

Yesenia finished reading and Jessica said, "The thing is, in this room we all understand," and then she read to us her story of being a fatherless girl, "feeling like a criminal myself when all I want is to be Daddy's little girl..." It was a story she had never told anyone before POPS.

When she finished, I asked both girls if they would read to the whole group next week. It takes courage to do that. There are usually 60 plus people in the room. But they both said, "Yes!"

"I might cry," Jessica said.

"That's okay," Yesenia told her.

"I'll cry," I told them. "I promise you," and that made them both laugh because they know how easily they make me cry.

"It's okay to cry in here," Yesenia said, "When I cry I look up and breathe really deep, and I see all those nice faces, and that usually makes me stop crying."

"Okay," Jessica said. "I'll read."

The next week she did, and these two young women and all these other brave, wise young people are sharing their stories. In these pages you'll read stories and poems by students from POPS the Club at Venice High, LA High School of the Arts and Lawndale High—POPS the Club is spreading around the country. The students of POPS Lumberjack High in Bemidji, Minnesota named this volume. And next year's volume will feature work from the students from all the new clubs—across southern and northern California, in Ohio and Texas and Washington State, and Virginia and New York.

And after you read them, you'll know what I know: That these are stories we all need to hear.

Amy Friedman, April 2016

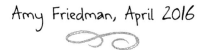

No one is born hating another person because of the color of his skin, or his background, or his religion. People must learn to hate, and if they can learn to hate, they can be taught to love, for love comes more naturally to the human heart than its opposite.

NELSON MANDELA
Long Walk to Freedom

Before There Were Bars

BY ALISON LONGMAN

Before there were bars
there were mothers, fathers, brothers, and sisters
there were cousins, aunts, uncles, grandparents, godparents,
and neighbors
there were friends and classmates.

Before there were bars
there were family dinners and first days of school
there were birthdays and holidays and summer nights spent
together
there were bedtime stories and kisses good-night.

Before there were bars
there were basketball games and dance practice
school performances and graduation ceremonies.

Before there were bars
there were smiles and warm embraces
and laughter.

Before there were bars
there were families.

And even with the bars
there is love.

Locks & Keys

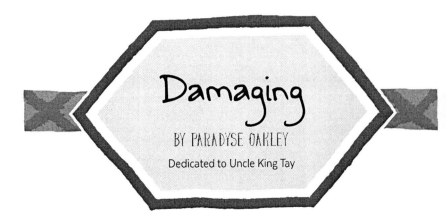

Damaging

BY PARADYSE OAKLEY

Dedicated to Uncle King Tay

Uh oh, not again.
　　You're locked up in the pen
For what this time
You don't even want us to know.
You're locked up in the pen
How do you think that makes us feel?
You have kids now, and nieces and nephews looking
Up to you.
You're locked up in that pen
What can we do?
Only pray that this time is the last.
But how can that be true when this is a system
That was never made for us.
Uh oh, you're locked up in the pen.

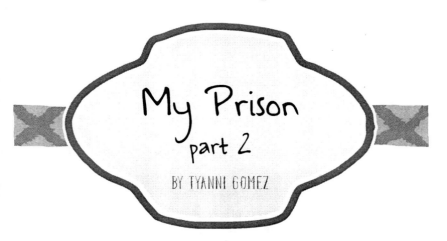

My Prison
part 2
BY TYANNI GOMEZ

S hattering in this pain
I'm almost out of this pain.
My emotions are becoming better.
I am becoming wiser and stronger.
I'm almost out of this pain.
My stressful situations are gone.
The person who sent me to this prison.
I'm almost out of this pain.
The person who played with my emotions.
The person who promised "forever and ever" was a lie.

I'm starting to release myself out of this prison.
I'm starting to be myself again.
I'm starting to forget the past.
The past that was haunting me.

Sitting down.
I look to my left...a life behind that wall.
I look to my right...a life behind that wall.

"Just pick yourself up"
I say to myself.

I stand.

The doors are open.
I'm out and I'm free.

TYANNI GOMEZ
Portrait by Chris Wright

Hurt

BY PARADYSE OAKLEY

Why am I hurting?
I know the real reason
I just don't want to admit it
How's my household
Dysfunctional?
Is it because my dad is incarcerated?
Oh

Okay, it's supposed to
Be a mom and dad
Not just one
They live in a society
Where you see that
Every day
At least one has been lost to
The system
Pa

In the Prison System
What I've been feeling is
A System that was made to
Incarcerate
People like me
Don't believe that
History

One Morning, Nine Years Ago

BY MAYNOR GALLETAN

A long time ago my family was involved in a lot of negative things. These negatives have left many of my family members and me scarred and afraid of drugs and the problems they bring. Afraid of gangs and the lives they take, not necessarily in deaths, but with mistakes that change people's lives forever.

Early one morning, nine years ago.

I awake on my parents' bed. I am swept from a deep sleep from a conversation between my mother and father. I crack open my eyes to see my father rushing to pull on his clothes and my mother sitting motionless on the bed, a frantic tone in her voice.

Due to my drowsiness I can't decipher what they are saying. My father flees the room. My mother remains inert. I stay still trying to comprehend the situation.

Soon I hear noises coming from outside of our house. I leap from the bed and hurry to the window. When I peek out I see a man dressed in all black pointing an M-16.

I have seen guys like this before on TV, chasing bad guys. But the sight of a pointed weapon just feet away fills me with fear. And it freezes me.

My mother shouts and pulls me away from the window.

I hear the guy with the automatic weapon shout, "Come out with your hands up. We have him in custody."

I think, "Who's him?" And, "Who are they talking about?"

My mother holds my sister's hand and leaves the house. I look over our driveway and I see the person I love so much, the "him in custody" with a look of sadness and terror on his face.

That image is burned inside my brain. I am unable to erase it, though I've tried. That one frozen image carried with it the promise of a massive and inexplicable change that was on the way.

But often I look back and examine that image. That frozen moment in time. And yet it changes as I grow older and mature.

Now, at 17, a senior in high school, a good student, a star football player, I ask, "Was it all for the good?" And, "What if I had chosen the same path, the wrong path, my father took?" And, "What if the same gangs and drugs that took my father away had taken me to the similar places, to a similar fate?"

I feel as if I am meant to make a difference. To break the chain. To follow a better path.

Although these thoughts roam freely in my mind, I can't help but wonder what it would have been like to grow up with a father beside me.

The Dream

BY JUANITO HERNANDEZ

I meet a man in a dark room.
Just me and him in a tiny room.
A bit of light standing between us.
We stand and stare for a moment.
Face to face. Eye to eye. Silent.
Questions running through my head.
Why am I even here?
Who is this man? I've never seen him before.
What does he want from me?
He speaks to me in a deep voice, saying,
"I am your blood, your grandfather."

We shout harsh words at each other.
Evil vibes bounce back and forth around the room.
I say he wouldn't dare hit me. He does.
He tests me and says I won't hit him back. I do.
It's quiet. No words at all.
We stare at each other with much pride.
He speaks softly and slowly. He says,
"If I turn my back on you, you die.
But if you turn your back on me first, I die.
Your choice…"

As if he knew the most important thing about me.
I wouldn't take the life of another human being.
I am nervous, sweating, and thinking.
What if he turns around first?
One minute…two minutes…three minutes…
Every minute that passes by feels like an eternity.
I wake up. What a horrible dream.

Ten years later…
January 12, 2016. 6:47 p.m.
I hear a voice.
"So we meet at last…"
I meet the man in my dream.
My grandfather, recently released from prison.
Charged for murder. Sentenced to 35 years.
He claims he is innocent and was framed.
Should I trust this man I've never met?
Should I believe what he says?
Or should I turn my back on him?

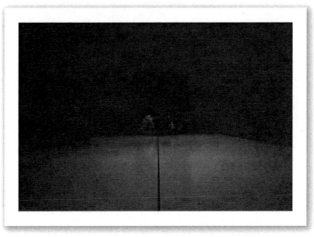

THE LOOK OF MY DREAM
Juanito Hernandez

I Forgive You

BY MADISON ABERCROMBIE

My love was pure
My mind was innocent

Roses are red violets are blue
You took my heart, as they took you

I went from being an innocent little girl to being the daughter
of a criminal
I went from being "daddy's little girl" to "your father doesn't
love you."

You destroyed me
Everything I did was to prove myself to you
I got all good grades
I even spoke badly of Mom, hoping you would accept me as
your little girl again

I drank like you did
I smoked like you did, so when you got out of jail you could
see how much of you I was like

You are the reason I don't trust anyone anymore
The reason I am afraid to get close to anyone

You hit my sisters and me for no reason, and then, when you
woke up from your nap, You forgot why our faces were bruised,
You forgot why your handprint was imprinted on our faces
You told us you were sorry, then the next day you hit us again
if we asked you why we couldn't get out of our room

You took my childhood away
You hit Mommy in front of us and told her we were nothing
I hated the way you treated us, but I still prayed to god for you
to love me
I still cared about what you thought
I still cried when they came to take you away

You went to jail, I wrote to you
You never wrote back
I'm sorry, Daddy

You walked away and didn't come back
Was I not a good enough daughter?
Was I a disappointment?
Am I really not worth it?

When you got out you said sorry
We became closer, but only until I ran out of money
I gave you money for beer
I gave you money for cigarettes

You found another woman
Who said I didn't deserve you

Who said I didn't deserve to be an Abercrombie
You believed her and you stopped calling me to say goodnight

I went from being a daddy's girl and playing catch every day
with my beloved father to
Being a no good, rebellious child
I went from being Madison Rae to being whatever people
knew me as...
I went from being a girl who accepted life as it was to being
distraught and angry at the world

You say you didn't do anything, but we both know that's a lie
But somehow it's ok
And somehow I can say I forgive you

Me experiencing you drinking 9-10 bottles of beer a day
Me experiencing you hurting my beloved mother
You breaking my heart more and more since I was 8
You made me a survivor, so thank you, Daddy
Thanks for giving up on me
Because now I know what not to do
So, Dad, I forgive you.

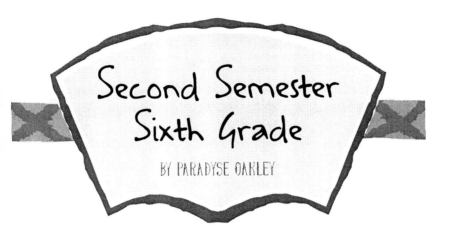

Second Semester Sixth Grade

BY PARADYSE OAKLEY

S econd semester of sixth grade, you went in
Praying every day and night that you would come home.
I remember searching your name, but the results were not
what I had expected.

Two years later I graduated High Honor Roll just wanting to
make you smile from ear to ear.
Every Saturday or Sunday driving to see you
I was happy and loved telling you about my week
Hoping that you'll see me graduate from middle, high school
or college
I will stay strong and focus on school, like you said.
Fast forward three years
I'm a junior at Lawndale, top 10% of my class of 2017
Hoping that next year you'll see
Me cross the stage
Making you proud will always be on
The top of my list
Fast forward one year

My senior year, will you be there or not?
I don't want to cross the stage and
Not see your face on the track.
Will I need to go to jail in my cap and gown?

WHERE THE HEART IS

My House Was Empty

BY RANDY CHAVEZ

My house was empty
My father gone working multiple jobs to keep us having food
I remember my father's two-story house,
big yard,
pigs and sheep, five dogs

That was the ranch where we
played cops and criminals
we had walkie-talkies that didn't work
it was a huge plot of Mexican soil
and it was fun
but when I turned 6

Dad got us US papers
and we moved to Venice, California
I didn't feel empty or alone
because my dad was with me
a hardworking electrician

My mother worked hard, too
After she dropped us off at school
she cooked, cleaned and did laundry all day

She also cleaned my uncle's house
and at 2:30 she waited for me outside my elementary school
we walked to nearby Mark Twain Middle School to pick up my
brother

Two years later we moved to 99th Street in Inglewood
never expected our neighbor would shoot at the cops
but he did

Four years later we moved again
75 miles north to Lancaster
There we added a new member of the family,
My sister-in-law

We only lasted two years there
We moved 50 miles south to Sun Valley
Where we've added another new member to our family
My niece who is always running around
messing up the living room

Every day around six
I'd watched my father struggling to take off his work boots
my mom cooking
sister-in-law helping
oldest brother lying down in his room
watching movies, waiting to be called to the table for dinner

My middle brother, as usual, showered, dressed and sped off in his Jeep
gone with his friend Luis to record some TV show about music
I'm the youngest
I flop down on the sofa and watch YouTube videos
Sometimes my niece comes in and bothers me

I don't know how I'll react when my brother moves in next month
He has twin girls.
The family will grow
So far, so good

What I hate is that I've have always lived near airports
LAX, General William F. Fox Airfield in Lancaster, and now Bob Hope Airport in Burbank
The constant groaning of engines and squealing of tires is annoying
There's never any real peace

But the one thing I know for sure,
The one thing that matters most
is that I'll always keep my family near me
no matter how we grow
or where our next move takes us

RANDY CHAVEZ
Portrait by Chris Wright

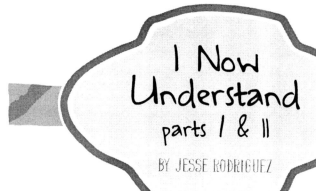

I Now Understand
parts I & II

BY JESSE RODRIGUEZ

PART I

I wanna shout WHY

15 years of marriage now I have to see my father go

Love? Loyalty? Where'd it all go?

I wanna shout WHY

You made it 15 years why couldn't you go another 15 years?

I remember my mom always tried to explain it to me but it went in one ear and out the other

I wanna shout WHY

but no matter how many why's, how's, and when's I was just a little kid

I always felt like it was my fault for all the things I did

I wanna shout WHY

But why? I will still feel the pain running through my veins

My heart will still ache and break each time I see my dad and he drives off to his other home

I wanna shout HELP

Because the rain still comes and I feel as if the sun's never going to come

But I'm grown, I'm 18 I now understand
I'm still both of your guys' biggest fan
I wanna say Thank You
For I knew
You guys had your reasons
Each day was like our 4 seasons
All the screaming, all the cussing and fussing, I don't think I
would've made it
another 15 years either
But
He's still my father.
And you're still my mother

PART II

I was maybe around eight
Little, short, chubby kid always wanting to go home late
Even when home didn't feel like home, I still had hope
Maybe one day, my home would be silent and peaceful
I would walk home, slowly... Asking myself millions of ques-
tions...Why...Why?
At times I would want to cry
Why lie
The closer I got to the house, the closer it felt like hell
Well...
It was quiet
For once...
Not for long.
Less than a second and it felt as if they flipped a switch and
the Lion was fighting a Lion.

All the screaming!
I'd lie in bed wondering if everyone went through this, or was
I just dreaming?
Was it my fault they argued? Was it because of school, the fact
that my grades weren't the best like the other little kids?
Or was it...because of all the stupid things I did?
It didn't make sense
Anger built and built up like ashes on an ash tray
I came to a conclusion and blamed Mom
All the unfitting, awful words I'd say to her
All because I blamed her...

I'm grown. I'm 18, and I now Understand.

I Remember

BY YESENIA GOMEZ

Remember when you could sit on your father's lap and cry like there was no tomorrow? I remember my dad's lap used to be my favorite and safest place in the world. He was the one I would run to after school. He was the one who attended all my parent conference meetings. He was the one who taught me how to add and subtract and how to read and write. He was the one who bought me everything I asked for. He was the one who took me to the park and played tag with. He was the one who attended all my school performances. He was the one who would take me to the doctor's office every time I was ill. But, he was also the one who caused me the most pain in my very early years. He was the one who would touch me in places I wasn't supposed to be touched. He was the one I had to go press charges on. He was also the one I loved even after what he did to me.

I remember the day I pressed charges on him. It was also the day I went to a foster home because my mom had a mental disorder. I remember being dragged out of the police station by a man I didn't know. I remember walking into a big white van. Maybe that's the reason I don't like vans. I remember crying for my mom and thinking, "She doesn't love me. If she

did, she wouldn't have left me here at the police station. She knows I am scared of them."

I remember all three of the foster homes I used to live in. The first was by 42nd street. I remember that the only friend I had at the school was one lunch lady who looked like my aunt. My second foster home was by 10th street. I didn't have friends there, not even a lunch lady. I had haters. I was the girl with straight, light brown hair and the one the teachers hated for talking too much. I wasn't talking though, I was defending myself verbally from two girls who would bully me every day. My third foster home was in Northridge one block away from the E.T. Park. I remember I only had one friend in that school. Her name was Michelle. She was another seven-year-old, just like me. Except she lived with her mom and dad. I was only her friend because she would share her lunch with me. That makes me sound like a bad person, but I was seven, and I was hungry. The only thing I liked about that school was tetherball. I would challenge the girls and boys from my class, and the winner received a dollar from the loser. I always won. I would use that dollar to buy a snack or water.

I remember everything. I remember the phone calls that I received from my mom and dad. I remember the visits every fifteen days. I also remember that all the phone calls and visits had to be supervised by the foster mom. I remember talking in code to my mom and telling her how much I hated my foster parents. I remember her telling me I would be with her soon. That soon didn't happen until two years later. I remember being back with my mom. But it felt like I was the mom all over again.

Christmas

BY ANGELA HERNANDEZ

Isn't Christmas supposed to be about families getting together and sharing

Laughter and joy?

Well, my Christmas was awful.

Mom and Dad screaming at me because they can't stand having me around.

Giving me looks as if they want to grab me and beat me to death.

I know I made a lot of mistakes, but there's no need to make me feel worse.

I don't feel like I'm part of this family anymore.

Too much pain.

Christmas is ruined for me.

All I want is for my family to show me a little bit of love

That there's no need to hold a grudge. I'm just a kid.

Christmas is ruined for me.

There's Always a Reason

BY DAISY LOPEZ

Ain't it crazy how it all started? One moment you see nothing, the next you wake up in a room full of your loved ones. Growing up thinking your life is perfect, but is it really? Once you hit the worst moments, it's like BOOM! That's where reality comes from. Once you hit high school you know who you are and where you stand.

I'm not here to tell you what life consists of, I just want you to hear me out, to listen to what I've been through.

I was the youngest of four, always getting picked on, being left out of everything. Being the youngest is tough; people think if you're the youngest, you get spoiled or you're more loved than the others are. But my family isn't like that. My family made me feel left out, especially once my niece came into this world. I love her. I might not show it, but she's also my world, but once she came, I was jealous. I'd do one little thing and get in trouble. Once we had visitors over to the house; my mom used to work at KFC, and you know everyone loves fried chicken. So I warmed up some chicken and started feeding my visitors. My niece wanted some, but I told her to hold on, to let me feed my visitors first. So she cried to her mom, my older sister, just like she always did, and she came at me, loud.

So I got loud, too. I said, "I didn't give birth to your child so why do I have to be responsible for feeding her?" My sister got mad and was ready to smack the food out of my hands, and I thought, Why me? I pushed my niece and told her to move, and she told my dad who got mad and hit me in front of all my visitors.

Looking back at that moment, I question myself. Did my actions call, "Yell at me, hit me, treat me like nobody"?

My brother, Jordan, is my biggest fear. He's been in and out of jail since he was 15. I was just a baby then, and I didn't know how cruel or tough life was. No one understands the pain I feel inside. I barely spent time with Jordan or talked to him, and that was hard. Bianca, one of my sisters, and I would wake up to banging on the front door. We didn't know what was going on. My parents ran downstairs and as always, there were the cops asking for Jordan, asking where he was.

Jordan was in his room, sleeping, doing absolutely nothing, but they rushed into his room and started asking questions. Sometimes they took him away. Every time he'd go to jail, I would ask my parents where he was, but they never told me.

I don't understand how people put their lives at risk. Who wants to live in prison or die? I just don't get it. People in gangs or crews have family to look after, but it's as if they're saying to us that they don't care about us. Every parent loves their children, even if they don't show it. My mom doesn't show her love or affection; she can be a harsh woman. She speaks her mind, and I think that's where I get it from. I don't show my emotions. But I have them.

There is so much more that goes on in my life, but I can't say it all. I just wanted to say some of it. I'm always smiling, I look happy, but that doesn't mean I'm ok. I just don't want to show my emotions because I don't want people judging me or being rude about my past.

Not everyone's life is perfect. If you care about your surroundings, you should ask people about their lives. You should try to talk to them. You should try to make them feel welcomed.

This is a little poem I wrote about Jordan.

They say there is a reason,
They say that time will heal,
But neither time nor reason
Will change the way I feel.
No one knows the heartache in me
That lies behind my smile,
No one knows how many times,
I have broken down and cried.
I want to tell you something,
So there won't be any doubt,
You're wonderful to think of
But so hard to be without...

Home is Not Smelling Cherry Pie

BY MADISON ABERCROMBIE

Home is not walking through the door and smelling cherry pie.
Home is a policeman dressed as a pizza delivery-man and taking my dad "for a drive."
At least that's what my mom said.

Home is not coming home every day to a home cooked meal.
Home is coming home to an empty house with a microwave and bread.

Home is not a big two-story house.
Home is on the second floor with a bedroom for Mom and another for me and my sisters.

Home is not with a loving, hardworking dad.
Home is, "Daddy will be back later, baby."

Home is not with a happy, healthy mom.
Home is, "Mommy went in for surgery, make sure you save leftovers for the other two."

Home is not a different bike every other Xmas.

Home is uniform clothes every Xmas.

Home is with a hardworking, positive-minded, cancer-surviving
mom.
Home is with a drugged out, sad, dysfunctional dad
Angry at me and the world.

Home is home.

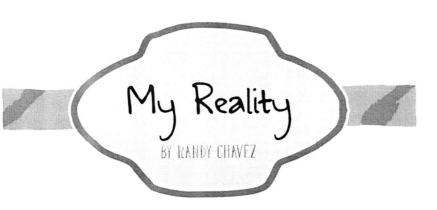

My Reality

BY RANDY CHAVEZ

I come from an ex-gang member father
And a short, beautiful mother
I come from a father who wears long sleeves
to cover up his ink

I come from two Hispanic parents
who bought empty lots from my grandpa
so there was some money in his pockets

I come from helping build five family houses in Mexico
for my brothers and me
but still renting in America

I come from a father who works from 5 a.m. to 8 p.m.
or later
so he can provide his family with the basics

I come from Mexico
where we could not imagine a good future
I come from drinking from 8 a.m. to 2 p.m.
while thinking about life
or maybe trying not to think about life

I come from middle of the night walks
dark streets and through empty lots
I come from not eating
because I was too busy drinking

I come from Mexico
where you know people
who ended up in a dark room
tied to a chair

I come from Mexico
where my real bros still live
waiting for me to return and throw
a New Year's Eve party

I come from two Hispanic parents
who grow annoyed by their sons fighting
their sons who love one another

I come from a f—ed up world,
Yet I am happy for what I have
and will find my path to success
because I know God is always with me

And yes, this is my reality.

MOTHER & CHILD

I am the Mother of My Mother

BY MADISON ABERCROMBIE

I am the mother of my mother
I wonder if I will ever get the chance to be a child
I hear my mother cry in pain and throw up her food
I see my mother grow thinner and lose her hair day by day
I want to be able to say, "My mother is healing."
I am the mother to my mother
I pretend she is my child
I feel that we have grown stronger
I touch my mother's forehead as she catches another fever
I worry that my mother won't get the chance to see me grow up
I cry when I see my sister realize her mom's health isn't
improving
I am the mother to my mother
I say, "You are strong enough to continue fighting.
I dream that you do not have cancer."
I try to be a daughter, student and sister
I hope that my mother loves me enough to want to keep
fighting
I am the mother to my mother.

Life Changed

BY NICHOLE LANDAVERDE

Regardless of the circumstances, what happened last year changed my life for the better. Walking towards the car where my mother was waiting after school on April 25, 2015, the sun felt warm on my shoulders. The sun was shining brightly at 3 o'clock. We drove off, heading to my grandma's house as we usually did on a Thursday evening.

When we arrived, my mother headed straight to my grandma's room. She always watched *Law and Order* when she was not working. I headed towards the kitchen, hungry after not eating at school. I asked my mother if she wanted me to make soup. She said yes. After the soup was warm, I handed it to my mother. We ate in separate rooms–due to the TV channel issue.

Minutes later my aunt and grandma walked in, aimed for the kitchen. I was focused on the channel, my feet kicked up on the coffee table, when I heard a scream from my aunt. "Call 911." The way her voice cracked made my stomach turn, the way it does when you know nothing good will come after. I made it halfway down the hallway when my aunt blocked my path into the room. 911 was on the phone by that time, I overheard my aunt telling the paramedics why she was calling. I was clueless when she hung up, I needed answers. She calmed down and explained. "Out of nowhere your mom turned pale and is having a hard time taking in air." At first I convinced myself it was not a big deal. She had visited the ER multiple times, but it was never fatal.

Outside the paramedic's van was flashing red lights, and they walked in with a gurney. I was in the living room when she was headed outside, accompanied by the paramedics. She was conscious, but her eyes were closed. She was pale as paper, and she definitely did not look well. She was not shaking or making eye contact. In a way she looked ashamed for being in this condition. I fought my way into the ambulance to join her. She looked at me with no clue as to who I was and began to mumble. "Why is this happening to me?"

I did not have an answer. How could I? She looked hopelessly at me, with more confusion than I felt. The feeling was overwhelming. I couldn't accompany her to the hospital.

I do not regret it. I would not have helped. I couldn't even begin to imagine what she was feeling. I told her I would see her later, and we left it at that.

I informed my father since he was at work. I knew he would rush straight to the hospital. I did not tell him to pick me up. I don't do well under difficult circumstances, especially if I can't do anything to help. It was 11 p.m., and I had not heard from anybody. I was still at my grandma's house with my grandpa. I had gone to the bathroom more than ten times. What could I say? I was nervous.

I called my father for an update, but each time I heard only the answering machine. Five minutes later I received a text. Deep inside I knew that was not a good sign, but I ignored the feeling. "We will be there in five minutes," I read. I knew "we" wasn't him and my mother but him and everybody else.

The door was slowly opening when my three aunts and my father walked in. Red, big, puffy eyes was all I focused on. I knew why. My father told me anyway, and I let him. I needed to hear the words. No tears ran down my face; I was in shock.

I didn't blame anyone. I understand that we live to die. But man, did it hurt. Mainly because, in addition to her being my mother, she was amazing. I wanted to be like her—to have her personality. She was so different from my father. I will never get over the fact that I was 13 when I lost her. I feel stupid for not getting closer to her when I had the chance.

The evening became even more painful when my brother arrived. He was two hours away, in Santa Barbara. I saw him two full hours after I found out. He knew when I saw him. When I saw him, he brought out the tears that I had been holding in. He moved closer to hug me. I didn't want to be touched, but his touch was all right. I sat in the same place, same position, as I watched people walk in and out of my grandma's door. It was 3 a.m.

That day was memorable, and it hurts still to think about it, but it made me realize that everyone has issues and everyone copes differently with their emotions. I want to study psychology, social behavior, including human development. I want to understand how an event can affect a person's thoughts. Losing my mother helped me appreciate the people I choose to surround myself with. Don't get me wrong, the sorrow hits me at random times, but I know it all happened for a reason.

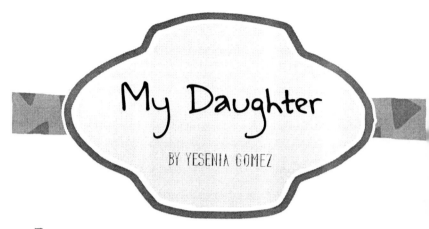

My Daughter

BY YESENIA GOMEZ

I was a mother at the age of eight. I took care of my 28-year-old mother.

The first of every month was something I craved. Those were the days she actually took care of me. My mother suffered from schizophrenia. I was starving for her attention and got it every month when we went to the grocery store because she received our Food Stamps.

My mother didn't and doesn't cook. She never learned because her mother died when she was nine. Since my mother didn't cook, everything she bought was canned or frozen. My mother wasn't a good mother, but I don't blame her. I blame the pills she took for her illness. I blame the government for taking me away when she needed me the most.

Although my mother didn't raise me for ten years, I love her with all her flaws and mistakes. She wasn't there for me when I needed her, and I wasn't there for her when she needed me. But now that we are together again, she is there for me and I am there for her.

I was a mother at the age of eight. My 28-year-old child isn't my child, she is a 36-year-old mother with a 16-year-old daughter.

Home with My Mom

BY MADISON ABERCROMBIE

As I laugh,
as I cry,
I know you always will know
that you are mine

As I cut myself
as I try to commit suicide
you show me how I'm strong
and that I should never hide

As he pulls my hair
and drives away
you are there
and there to stay

As I hit you
as I say, "I hate you,"
you laugh, then
you cry

I'm sorry I'm a disappointment
I'm sorry I get high

you try and try
and are always good to me

I laugh and leave
but never for long;
I'm not the first
to say goodbye

You're a good mom,
You're my best friend
I write and write
Your name will never be forgotten,
as long as I hold this pen

The Tattoo

BY MIRANDA HUGHES

Pain?

That was the last thing on my mind. I was more concerned that my father would find out that his 16-year-old daughter, his only daughter, was deep in the 'hood, sitting in a stranger's living room being tattooed, without his knowledge or consent.

But that didn't matter because once the needle pierced the upper left side of my bony shoulder and traced the curves of a capital "C," the first letter of my mother's name, I felt emboldened, powerful.

I felt the blood of my courageous mother running through me.

I felt a sense of pride that I would soon wear her name on my body.

"What letter are you on?" I asked the tattoo artist.

"The *h*," he said.

And as he spoke I started to feel the pain that accompanied the loop on the h, the letter closest to my collarbone.

I sweated. I squirmed.

Which led me to imagine the pain my mother must have gone through when I was seven years old and she, a young mother, knew she was dying and would leave her two children with her unreliable, alcoholic husband.

I fought through the pain.

"R, i, s, t."

The letters were being traced much faster now.

"Take slow, deep breaths," the tattoo artist said. "I'm working on the second *i*. We're almost done now."

My body trembled as he inked the last letter of my mother's name.

Finally, it was done.

He handed me a small vanity mirror so I could admire his finished product.

I loved the simple, flowing cursive letters that spelled "Christine," the name that represents strength, beauty and courage. The name of my mom who was taken from her daughter and from the world way too soon.

Every time I miss her, which is often, I touch the left side of my upper shoulder, near my heart, and I remember who the most important woman in my life was and still is.

And I know she is always with me.

MIRANDA HUGHES
Portrait by Chris Wright

MEMORIES OF OUR FATHERS

JOHN BEMBRY
Portrait by Doris Longman

My Father, My Homeboy

BY RANDY CHAVEZ

My father, my homeboy.
I look up to him.
At age 9, he lost his father.
And had to go to work to help support his two sisters, seven brothers and his mother. By eleventh grade he had to drop out to work fulltime and then some.

Two jobs.
One of his paychecks went to his mother; the other he kept for himself.
When he met my mother everything changed.
He dropped the gang life.
He worked harder.
Now he owns a ranch in Mexico and a few other properties.
His daily grind starts at 5 a.m. He's home around 7 at night.
Some don't understand how this former tough guy could have so much in life.

Every day when I wake I look at him and ask myself, "How can he not be exhausted?"

He gets mad when my teachers call and say that I talk too much in class.

He says, *"Quieres trabajar dia y noche no es facil? esta oportnidad que? no? menso?"*

"You want to work day and night? It's not easy. Take this chance that you have. Don't be dumb."

I listen to my father, my homeboy.
Why would I not believe him?

I Want My Daddy Back

BY LESLIE MATEOS

I want my daddy back
That's all I ask for.
To see him again
Hug him again.
Have him with me.
It's been ten years and no sign of him
No calls from him
Why?
Because he was deported after being in prison
They took him away from me.
He's scared of crossing the border.
He's scared of prison.
Will he ever come back?
I want my daddy back.
He's the only one missing in the pictures.
I've culminated from elementary school
I've culminated from middle school
I've graduated from high school
And I am determined to graduate from college

But will he be there?
Will he finally be in the picture?
I want my daddy back.

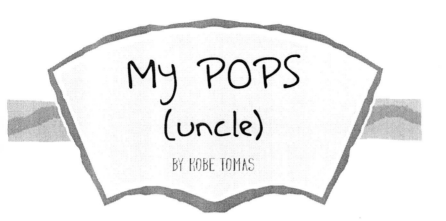

My POPS
(uncle)

BY KOBE TOMAS

As far back as I can remember he was my babysitter.
He was the first man I ever knew, taking care of a child
while he sipped his brew.
Taught me how to cook. Bought me my first book. Taught me
how not to be shook.
Never did like watching him beat my aunt or hurt my sisters.

One time things got out of hand, so my mom had to get in.
My POPS was laying hands on her too.
Then he got his brewskies and ran away.
A few minutes later the cops came. My aunt was crying.
That was the last time I saw him for a while.
He was caught and locked up for assault and other charges.
No one picked me up from school after that, so that's when I
learned to walk home from school by myself.

When he came out he looked different: skinnier and quiet.
Until he started drinking again.
When he started throwing up blood, he had to stop drinking
He ended up hospitalized and almost died on us three times.
This year I found out he needs a transplant that costs 18k.

I remember him telling me, "Everything's going to be okay." But ever since he stopped living with me things haven't been okay.

I have no father figure to look up to.

Broken Man

BY KATHERINE SECAIDA

Dad, is that you yelling at my mom?

Dad, are those your belongings in black bags outside the door?

Dad, is that you drinking and passing out on the couch?

Dad, I hid under the bed at the age of four because I was afraid of you.

Dad, is that you locked up?

Dad, is that you breathing in an inhaler installed in your car?

Dad, is that you in the hospital hooked up to all these machines?

Dad, where are you?

Dad, who are you?

Dad, what's next?

Dad, how long will I have you in my life?

Dad, I hear you say, "I love you, you're my little girl and I'm praying to God to let me live a little longer to see you grow just a little more."

But nothing is promised, Dad, because I don't have you.

You are a broken man with no way out.

You try to come back in, but I can't forgive you, but I can feel bad for having a broken father but feel strong about being raised by a strong woman playing your role
Mother and Father.

Perra Vida

BY ROSA ISELA RUIZ

Nunca he tenido
el calor de mi padre
ni el amor de esa persona
que se llama papá

Es difícil crecer sin un papá
Mirar a mis amigas que tienen un padre
Y que les digan hija o mi niña
es muy difícil para mí

También ver a mis primos
tener a su papá
Y los abrazan y les dan
ese calor de amor
Me imagino que es muy lindo

Es feo por pasar burlas, discriminación y humillaciones
en las escuelas
o con tu propia familia
por no tener un papa, es muy feo
y más cuando tu propia familia
te discrimina y te hacen feo
solamente porque no tienes un padre

Le pregunté a mi mamá
cuando yo tenía once años que quien era mi padre
Me dijo que no tenía la edad
para saberlo y que cuando cumpliera
18 años lo sabría

Hoy día tengo 17 años
y todavía pregunto
y no he tenido una respuesta
siempre cambia la conversación
A la vez estoy feliz por cumplir los
18 años para saber quién es mi padre
Pero a la vez asustada por cumplirlos porque
tengo miedo de saberlo

La verdad es que
no sé si me quiere o me rechaza
Pero lo único que quiero
es saber quién es y que
sepa que tiene dos hijas en este mundo

En la manera que no nací con un padre
y que creo que nunca lo tendré cerca mía
no me gustaría que mis futuros hijos
sufran lo que yo he sufrido
en esta perra vida
Siempre le he llamado
"perra vida" porque nacimos para sufrir
y por otras cosas
que me han pasado

Dog's Life

BY ROSA ISELA RUIZ

Never in my life
did I understand the warmth of my father
nor the love of this person
that is called papa.

It is very difficult to grow up without a dad
to see my friends who have a father
that calls them daughter or "my little girl"
It is very difficult for me.

Also seeing my cousins
have a father
and the hugs they get
this warmth of love
I imagine it is very beautiful.

It is horrible to experience the jokes, discrimination
humiliations in school
or from your own family
for not having a father, it is ugly
when your own family
discriminates and makes you ugly
all because you don't have a father.

I once asked my mother
when I was eleven, "Who is my father?"
She said I was not old enough
to know and when I turn
18 I can find out.

Today, I am 17 years old,
and I still ask.
And she never has a response
or always changes the subject.
I am happy to turn
18 this year to learn who my father is.
But I am scared too because
I am afraid to know.

The truth is that
I don't even know if he wants me or rejects me.
But the only thing I want
is to know who he is and for him to know that
he has two daughters in this world.

In the way that I wasn't born with a father
and that I believe that I will never have one,
I do not want my future children
to suffer what I have suffered
in this dog's life.
I always call it this
"dog's life" because we were born to suffer
and with other things
that have happened.

ROSA ISELA
Portrait by Chris Wright

When I was Fourteen

By Michelle Cardoza

My stepdad tried to kill my mother when I was 14. He was the only father I ever had. Never did I imagine being in this position. Never did I think our father-daughter relationship would break apart. Never did I think my lovely daddy could be capable of killing the woman I love and admire so much. I was daddy's little girl my whole life. I was close to him. I loved him. Now I don't know what I feel for him. I don't hate him nor do I love him.

It was an ordinary night, but he and my mother started arguing. He had hit my mother twice before, when I was younger. They always hated each other but tolerated one another for the sake of my sister and me. An argument turned ugly. His huge hands were around my mother's fragile neck, getting tighter and tighter. Her hands were in the air. She could not move from the shock. My sister and I began to hit him until, finally, he let her go. I ran to my room and tried to call 911. He grabbed my leg and took away all the phones.

I will never forget the evil glare in his reddened eyes. I saw that he was not himself; he was on something, and his actions and his voice were different from anything I'd ever seen or heard. He was not my dad, he was the devil.

I ran to my aunt's house and she called 911, but he had already left the house with my dog.

The police arrived at our house and asked what happened. They left to search for him and found him 20 minutes later. I could not look at him, I was so scared. I took my dog, and once we were back home, I cried while my cousin held me. I felt as my life had flipped upside down. I was devastated. My lovely father had become a psycho. He went to jail, but wasn't deported. That night I lost a dad.

He is no longer the man I adored. He's just a man who took care of me for 14 years. He is the man who was there when my real father wasn't. I thank him for raising me and always providing for all of us. To him, I am his daughter. I do not hate this man who ruined my life, but if I don't hate him at least a little, I feel as if he has won.

To this day I see him once a week. We have nothing to say to each other. I forgive him, but I will never forget what he did.

My stepdad tried to kill my mother when I was 14.

I Am His Reflection in the Mirror

BY LESLIE MATEOS

I am his reflection in the mirror
My eyes, my lips, my nose, my hair even my moles everything I got from my dad
A dad that I love and hate at the same time.

I love my dad because he gave me the best childhood any kid can ask for.
I hate him for beating my mom halfway to death, those were my worst moments.
I hate the fact that I look like him. I don't want to look like him.

When people at parties ask me, "Who's your dad?"
I am ashamed to answer because they know my dad is an alcoholic.
I simply answer "Rigoberto Mateos the son of Roberto Mateos."
They instantly say, "Oh you look so much like him."

It makes me mad because when they say that, it makes me feel like I am him
And I am him because his blood runs through me.

Every time I look at myself in the mirror I see him
The same way Simba saw his dad in the lake.
I am his reflection in the mirror.

Don't Answer Dad

BY KOBE TOMAS

The only father figure I remember is my dad drinking liquor.
First time I met him, I was four.
It was across the street from a gym, and he was smoking a cigarette
While I wondered why he ever left.
Even though we haven't met, it's been a few years since you left.
I'm not mad that you left, I'm mad that you knew where I was but never came to look for me.

As a lil' kid I thought everyone only had a mother. I didn't know what a father was. I didn't know I had brothers 'til I was nine. They weren't around much, and when they were, I wouldn't feel right. Nothing made sense to me.

I wondered why my dad had gotten locked up for DUIs. Or what a DUI even was, why he only called when he was wasted.

The second time I saw him was one night when he woke me and my mom coming in in the middle of the night. He had nowhere to go, so he spent the night.

I remember fake sleeping, one eye open. Waiting for the right moment to say hi.

I waited for him to fall asleep before I crawled out of my bed and slept next to him and thought about what we were going to do the next morning. I figured we would have breakfast like any ordinary family.

But time slipped away, and I woke on the floor in an empty apartment. Dad gone without a trace and Mom off to work at the same place she always worked.

That whole day I wondered if I had only been dreaming
And why he didn't say goodbye.

Fatherless

BY IVORI WYCHE

My life is filled with the deaths of loved ones.
I try to grasp it all, understand.
Sometimes I ask, "Why me? Did I do something wrong?"

With each death, I grow more numb.
First my dad, next my uncle,
more recently my brother

I have grown up without the father I've always needed.

I let the simple-minded boys run in and out of my life,
Always searching and searching for that father figure I never
had.

My anger rises.

I return to my fifth grade graduation.
I search the crowd.

I see him.
He's here!
In back.
Standing tall

Like an NBA center,
Wearing his butter-colored Timberlands.
But,
No.
My imagination tricked me.

He wasn't here.
I stood frozen
Then let it all go.
Fine to cry in front of others
Who cared what they thought?
I stood, still there, fatherless,
Destroyed.

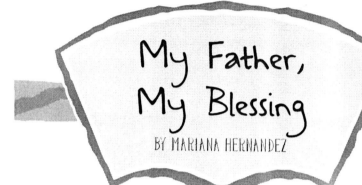

My Father, My Blessing

BY MARIANA HERNANDEZ

"My father once told me, *"Mija, tienes que estudiar muscho en escuel porque no quiere trabaja mucho como yo en el futuro."* Which means, "My daughter, you must study in school because you don't want to work hard in the future like me."

I look up to my dad for everything he's done for me, my sisters and our mom.

He never left our side and that's something for which I am grateful because most of my friends either don't have a father in their lives or they have a father who wants little or nothing to do with them.

I live to make my father proud of me. My goal is to become a pediatrician and as I have told him, "I'm going to make it to UCLA, pa. And it's all going to be for you."

For all 16 years of my life, my dad kept a roof over our heads and never hesitated to give his daughters whatever we needed, whether it was Barbies, books and supplies, or make-up.

And it's never been easy.

My dad has worked two jobs for the past 20 years. He leaves home at 4 a.m. to work in a UCLA cafeteria and when his shift ends at 2 p.m., he drives five miles to the Lowe's Santa Monica

Hotel where he works as a pastry chef. He usually returns home around 11:20 p.m.

It's painful to witness his struggle. It especially hurts because when he and his sisters left El Salvador and crossed the border, he was 16 and was unable to complete his high school education. In America, he immediately went to work as a waiter.

He always tells me not to worry about him and his work and to know that we, his daughters and his wife, are his blessings.

He has taught me to be kind to others and to find the good in people. And I like to think those words have shaped me into a generous and optimistic young woman who takes her friendships seriously and spreads a bit of cheer every day.

My father is always there, encouraging me, motivating me, showing me what it means to be a good parent. And I, in turn, feel a familial obligation to do well in school, to gain knowledge and wisdom and lead a life that will make my father proud.

Visiting Hours

My Visit

BY KATHERINE SECAIDA

Blank walls gray doors cold seats
Dirty glass windows
Phones dirty
Wet wipes to clean those sh____y ass phones
So silent that I can hear my heart beat
Your words to the phone don't even match the beat
Dad, your eyes are clearer, but how long will that be?
Your jumpsuit looks nice, how comfy is that?
You talk about the bed you sleep in
Cold small lousy made waiting just for you
Open your eyes
I'm rowing & I see all your dark sides
Dad, I love you, understand,
But don't expect me to always be your little girl
I grow every day. I don't need you.
It's fine that you were never there.
You put your hand to the glass to say your
Two-minute goodbye
And my heart just stops beating,
Cold-hearted, reminds me of the metal seats,
Don't touch anything
Shirt so dirty I don't even want to speak.

Right side there's a woman talking to her man with a child on
her chest
Child so close to the window pounding to break the glass to
reach to his dad
Left side there's a mother talking to her son
Reading the Bible and all I hear are her tears
Right in front of me there's a man who can hardly speak
Trying to keep his calm, watching his two daughters pick up a
phone for an hour conversation
Dad, you have five more minutes to speak
Say what you want to say but your words always repeat
As he hangs up, hand to glass to say goodbye
See what you did? Your daughters were right
You don't deserve them
As my mom repeats
Look at your girls, they're growing up
To not be half of your blood

KATHERINE SECAIDA
Portrait by Chris Wright

My First Visit in Prison

BY LESLIE MATEOS

My father was sent to prison for domestic violence when I was four years old. I missed him a lot and asked my mom where he was every single day. "When is daddy coming?"

My uncle Liborio called my mom two months later to inform her that he had arranged a visit for me to see my dad. My uncle told her that he'd come pick me up on Sunday morning. When my mom told me, "Leslie you're going to see your dad on Sunday. Your uncle is going to come and pick you up,"

I was happy to hear that. I spent the rest of the week making plans about what to tell the police so I could come back home with my dad.

I told my mom that I was going to have fun, that I was going to hug, kiss and sit on my dad's lap. She didn't say anything, just gave me a simple smile.

The week went by fast, and it wasn't long before my uncle came to pick me up. It was a long drive, but when we arrived I jumped out of the car eager to see my father, eager to hug and kiss him.

We stood in line for a while and while standing in line, I told my uncle about my plans. He didn't say anything. Once we got to the front of the line and passed into the visiting room I just saw a lot of people on the phone. A policeman came and took us to an empty chair. I sat down looking all over the room for my dad. Finally he came out; he was on the other side of the window. My uncle gave me the phone and told me to start talking. We had a small chat, but I started crying because it wasn't what I had imagined. I put my hand on the window, and so did my dad as to make it feel like we were holding hands.

That was my first visit in prison.

Photograph by Leslie Mateos

Fatherless Girl

BY JESSICA DE LA MORA

No father
no love
wondering if I matter
seeing my friends with their daddies
listening to classmates talk about their dads
how he took them to restaurants
and shopping malls
and told a boy something, defending his little girl

I'm lucky enough to remember him
his hugs
I mean, I think they're memories
either that or dreams
I remember playing Hide and Seek
with my dad and my sister
my dad and I hid in the bathtub
I couldn't stop talking and laughing
so the game didn't last long

My dad, to his daughters and family,
a big-hearted man
To others, a scary, tough criminal

tall, slim, bald, glasses, mustache
silhouettes of girls and gang signs inked into his arms and chest
In Corcoran State Prison,
Locked up since 2003
When I was four and my sister seven
Hearing about him getting out next year
or maybe the next
But I've been fed those rumors as far back as I can recall
Who knows when he'll be out?

I've heard so many stories
He's in for slanging drugs
for running from the cops
for violating his probation
I've never known the truth

I remember waking at 4 a.m. to visit him in prison
a four-hour drive to the middle of Nowhere, California
trees, plants, trains, abandoned houses
motels whose names I'd never heard of
staring out the window, no clue where I was
trying to sleep in the car
but too much on my mind for that to work

Standing outside the facility in the cold
trying to stay warm by hugging my aunt
who drove my cousins and me upstate

Prison guards
treating us somewhere between rude and disrespectful
all I want is to see my father

Waiting to hear, "De Le Mora, Mike."
passing through a metal detector,
being patted down
filling out forms
told what I can and cannot wear
no blue
no red
no designer clothes
no hoodies
no tight blouses
no short skirts
not too many layers of clothing
wireless bras only
Might as well go in naked
I never know what to wear
They always find something wrong
to give you a hard time
And steal away precious minutes from the visit

Then squished into a bus that creeks and lurches uphill from
station to station
dropping off visitors here
a few more there
Scared to make a wrong move, say the wrong thing

Makes me feel like I'm a criminal,
not someone's daughter
who only wanted to be daddy's little girl
for an hour or two
on a Sunday afternoon

FRIENDS INSIDE

Ordinary Weekend

BY JOHN RODRIGUEZ

As I sit there and dwell
my head spins while
trying to balance the worlds of love and hurt
She grabs my hands
and I don't know if she sees
that they're tattered and beat
but not physically.
I wonder if they look at me
and feel disgust for a fool covered in concrete.
They wait in long lines
And drive down miles of open road
to see if I will respond
and in a way learn to love again
and not be afraid to have friends
and not scared to show my feelings
but understand my life has meaning
besides simmering in a pool of iron
where boots clank and the years wave goodbye.
For these few seconds I have it under control.
A world is at ease

my hands sweat with remorse
and learn to ignore the hate and negativity that has
built up inside me.
But the speaker announces
that visiting is over.
I give a hug that I will miss
and spin away
from those
who make me feel like I'm worth living.
They smile but I know
it hurts them as much as it does me.
A feeling of gain and loss
a true oxymoron.
Out they go
back to their iron-touched lives
and I pass through the doorway
that leads to negativity.

The Letter

BY PAPA BEAR DE LA MORA

12/2/2015

Dear POPS,

Allow me a moment to share a bit about my life story in the system....

At the age of seven, I landed in the Juvenile Hall East Lake in downtown Los Angeles...stealing car stereos amongst other things was a quick way to make a dollar to buy my clothing, shoes and entertainment at the arcade in Next World at the UA Marina Del Rey. My parents bought me all any kid my age could wish for; well, I guess you can say I was ungrateful. I wanted more and was more concerned with impressing the girls and my homeboys. I was down for whatever and lookin' sharp all the time...Gangbangin' with the Homies turned violent when I picked up the gun for protection and drugs for slangin'...In and outta Juvenile Hall turned to LA County Jail, then State Prison, graduating with the Big Hogs. Ain't no more fist fighting in their neck of the woods—if you get called upon duty, it's with a knife or what we call a bone crusher, manmade prison knives...I used to enjoy earning my respect, putting in work for Our Cause...but after doing over 15 years in solitary confinement, I finally removed my blinders and saw things for what they truly are—I'm simply choosing my personal agenda over my family, and at the end of the day those homeboys, homies, whatever you call 'em, they will turn their backs on you in a heartbeat. Prison politics are nothing to play with...I prefer my family any day...breakin' the law will simply put you in jail and when you are on this side, you realize when it's too late that it's the family who truly matters. They hurt for you as well, and it's them who love and pray for you... Take it from my personal experience, Life of Crime is not the way to live...I had everything I could wish for on the streets, a bad ass beautiful wife who gave me two beautiful babydolls. But after all these years in and out of prison, it took a toll on our marriage and she filed for divorce. It was the worst feeling ever, I had just lost my mom who died from her longtime diabetes, and now to lose my wife after 15 years of marriage was devastating. All kinds of terrible thoughts ran through my mind...not giving a f___ what the consequences...while serving this time I've lost both my parents and two brothers and yet I was not able to attend their funerals due to being in prison. After my divorce, I made the decision to change my lifestyle and behave for my two babydoll daughters and my family who love and need me as much as I love and need them. I've gone from a test score of 2.4 to a 9.5 and soon will be taking my G.E.D. test and I'll be ready for the streets. If I've survived prison all these days, I know for damn sure I'll be good when I come home and with an education and willpower to live a life away from crime...My advice to

you all is to stay in school. Education is the true power and where all the real warriors are made.

Thank you for your time. Now get back to work.

Respectfully always,
Papa Bear
Merry Christmas to all and a safe happy New Year

Cayon

BY CALVIN CALLIER

She must have heard my voice
Coming through her grandmother's door
There atop 17 stairs,
Sitting on the first three that sat
at a right angle.
She couldn't have even been two
in nothing but her pamper.
"Daddy! Daddy! Daddy!" as she started to scoot.
"Bump." "Bump." "Bump," the familiar sound of her bottom
to the wood.
Phone pressed between my shoulder and ear,
the plastic handles of a grocery bag in one hand
and a stack of money in the other.
Good thing the groceries were light.
I had not yet looked up the stairs.
Only repetition and her voice told me
that she was still there.
The excitement in her voice
and the sound of "Bump" exceeding past three
caused me to look up
to find where she might be.
In looking up, I found her swinging her arms forward

thrusting her little thighs, she took flight,
How anxious!
How much trust!
"My Daddy won't drop me!"
Baby girl's got guts, plus she believed.
The thin plastic strap handles
pulled at my grip
limiting the use of my hands.
"My daughter's in the air and I've got to catch her."
This is real!
Her little body slammed against my chest
with a thump!
Her little hands clutched at my thin jacket top.
Her little feet gripped at my belt like hands.
Her head bumped my chest and she said "Oh!"
But I had her that's real,
she even said, "My Daddy got me," breathily.
She knew I'd catch her.
I knew nothing,
It was too quick.

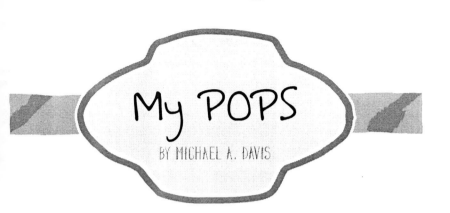

My POPS

BY MICHAEL A. DAVIS

I titled this piece "My POPS" because my pops (my father) is who I blamed for my having to experience the Pain of the Prison System in the first place.

My biological father spent nearly all my childhood years in prison. My biological father was a heroin addict who chose drugs, prison, and the criminal lifestyle over me. Prison and drugs were more important to him than I was. At least that's how I saw it....

When my biological father wasn't in prison, he *still* wasn't in my life. He chose to be a deadbeat dope-fiend rather than a decent, dependable dad. My biological father didn't love me. He didn't want to have anything to do with me. At least that's how I saw it....

When I was sexually abused by a stranger at the age of five, my biological father wasn't there to protect me. When I was sexually abused a second time by a stranger at the age of nine, my biological father wasn't there to protect me. When I was constantly physically and verbally abused by my stepfather throughout my childhood, my biological father wasn't there to protect me. At least that's how I saw it....

Not only is that how I saw it, it's also the way I felt about it. It's also the way I improperly processed all those damaging thoughts and hurtful feelings that came along with experiencing trauma at such a young age. Yeah, I think it's fair to say that the *PAIN OF THE PRISON SYSTEM* has negatively impacted me for my entire life, literally.

Today, at the age of 47, I ask myself how different might my life have been had my biological father been a part of it? I sometimes wonder, *Would I have been a college graduate with a great career and a beautiful family instead of a convicted felon serving a life sentence; a man who has spent most of my life in juvenile jails and adult prisons? Would I have been a good and decent father to my only child? Or would I be the father who thinks he's good and decent even though I've been locked up for my own child's entire life?*

I'd like to think that my life would have turned out much better had my biological father been actively involved in my life in a positive and productive manner, rather than a negative and destructive manner. At least that's how I see it....

The saddest part of this whole thing (the pain of the prison system), for those of us who <u>choose</u> to immerse ourselves in the criminal lifestyle while knowing that going to prison is a likely possibility, is that we don't take into consideration the profoundly negative impact that our decision-making is going to have on the ones closest to us, the people we say we love most. We don't think about the likelihood of leaving our children out there, unprotected, where they may potentially become victims of abuse or become so severely traumatized by the damaging void our absence creates that they grow up

suffering from overwhelmingly negative feelings and destructive perspectives of themselves.

Sadly, it doesn't even enter into our mindless equation that the children we leave behind may very well become so messed up in the head and heart that they might blindly, inadvertently, follow in our footsteps, all the way up to the prison's front door....

Obviously, it goes without saying, we victimize the people we commit our crimes against as well as their loved ones. But those of us in prison don't take into consideration the fact that we are also victimizing our own loved ones when we <u>choose</u> to commit crimes that lead to our going to prison. I emphasize the word <u>choose</u> because it is a <u>choice</u> that we make when we decide to commit the crimes which bring us to prison. We <u>choose</u> a life of crime over *them* (our family and loved ones). F__ it, ain't no sense in lying about it, the truth is, we <u>chose</u> our immediate feelings over our loved ones' long-term concerns. It's sad but it's true, and if you're mad about that, then it's only because the truth hurts you.

One of the things I've come to learn a lot about during my incarceration is INSIGHT. INSIGHT as to why I was so messed up while growing up. INSIGHT as to why I acted out in such a damaging and destructive manner while growing up. INSIGHT as to why I grew up acting out so violently as a teenager and young adult. Throughout the process of my gaining this insight, I discovered how profoundly negative a role my father, my POPS, and my stepfather played in my life....

My problems started with the fact that my biological father was in prison and not in my life. His not being there left me in a dysfunctional situation. The choices *he* made left *me* vulnerable to an abusive stepfather. I was beat mercilessly with any and everything my stepfather could get his hands on. I was verbally and psychologically abused. When I was five and six years old, whenever I cried too much after a vicious ass whoopin', my stepfather forcefully placed me behind the refrigerator. I remember being strung up and hung from the second floor banister, my stepfather's way of threatening and intimidating my mother by torturing me. I was brutally terrorized throughout my childhood, and because of these traumatizing events, I felt many feelings that as a child, I didn't know how to cope with: Fear, shame, hurt, humiliation, feeling unloved, feeling unwanted, helplessness, feeling powerlessness, feeling abandoned, feeling terrified, and feeling frightened which in turn led me to feeling distrust, hate, bitterness, and resentment. But above all else, I felt anger—hostile, hateful and destructively aggressive anger that eventually turned into uncontrollable rage.

In my young mind, I felt like my biological father didn't give a damn about me, and my stepfather hated me so much he wanted to destroy me, literally. So I grew up not giving a damn about me and subconsciously hating myself so much I wanted, literally, to destroy myself.

Thoughts form our feelings, and our feeling form our beliefs, and those beliefs ultimately determine our actions....

I thought I was worthless, useless, powerless, helpless, and hopeless. My thoughts caused me to suffer through some foul feelings which ultimately caused me to adopt a corrupt belief system. The dehumanization I was forced to endure at home led me to forcing others to suffer unfair victimization once I left the home. This was my way of projecting my pain onto

others and regaining all that I felt or thought was being taken away from me when I was a terrorized child. My foolish, selfish, thoughtless, and destructive actions eventually led me to being locked up for 33 of the 47 years that I've been alive.

When I share this story, people often comment with empathy and tell me I didn't have a chance. In a way they're right; I didn't have a chance. But what I did have was a *choice*. Unfortunately for me, and for so many others, I made a wrong choice too many times, choices that caused damage and that hurt a lot of people.

So, I say to those of you who are in any way, shape, or form experiencing the pain of the prison system: Make the right choices in spite of whatever it is that you are going through. Don't be afraid to express your thoughts and your feelings and your pain creatively through writing. Writing can be so therapeutic. Write and realize your fullest potential. Don't ask yourself, "Why me?"

Trust me, I understand your Pain of the Prison System. Now I hope you can understand mine and learn from it...

On behalf of all the fathers, sons, brothers, cousins, uncles, and nephews that are in or have been in prison, I offer my sincerest apologies for the pain that we men have caused each and every one of you to endure as a result of our foolish, selfish, thoughtless, and destructive actions. I offer my sincerest apology for our <u>choosing</u> *our* immediate feelings over *your* long-term concerns, and the ripple effects that have, and will, occur as a result.

The poem that follows, *Alone With My Thoughts,* is my therapeutically creative expression of the pain and anguish that

I experienced, and the path I traveled that led to where I am today.

ALONE WITH MY THOUGHTS

It wasn't until I was alone with my thoughts
That it all materialized, and I finally realized
That for so long, I had been so wrong, and so gone!
I walked around full of hate with a rock hard, fragile façade
My middle finger to the world with a mean-mug mask and an angry nod
My erratic emotions would give way to the chaotic thoughts festering in my mind
Then, mentally, I'd eventually, find myself in places so cruel and unkind
Feeling like a wild young animal violently stalking my cage
Silently suppressing my childish and hostile, savage-like rage
"Why was I so mad?" I asked, "Why was I so sad?" I asked,
"Why was I so bad," I asked
Oh shit!
Then it hit me like a ton of bricks!
The answers hit me relentlessly, continuously, causing me to flash!
As images of a violent childhood full of evil abuses emphatically splashed
Across the back of my tightly closed eyelids like a horrific car crash
My innocence lost at too young an age
My wholesome young heart corrupted and filled with an insatiable rage

Tremendously traumatic events caused me to form f__d up feelings unable to be assuaged

Countless incidents of violent senselessness dragged me down a destructive road, rough, rugged, and unpaved

I was just a child! I didn't deserve your vile! I didn't deserve your evil introductions! I didn't deserve your foul!

Five years old, my innocence maliciously ripped from me

Only to be brutally terrorized by a wickedly cruel stepfather, for years,

My self-worth viciously stripped from me!

Hurt people hurt people!

So my unfair f__in' pain was all you sonofabitch's was ever gon' ever get from me.

Aaaggghhh! Pop! Pop! Pop! Pop! Pop! Pop! Pop! Pop! Pop! Pop!

I showed my hate-filled bullets to the world until the entire clip was on empty

I hid my hurt for years. While I did my dirt for years.

And I did it all like it was nothing

My middle finger stayed on that self-destruct button.

But then a light came on, and it shone on somethin'

My decency! My integrity! My truest, most beautiful inkling of an identity!

That thug ain't me! That bad ass bastard ain't who I was born to be! Hell no! This prison life ain't gon' be my legacy!

That's when I looked deep within, and searched long and hard as I thoroughly explored who I really am

I cracked that rock hard fragile façade I once proudly and boldly strolled with

Just like an enemy code, I deciphered that confounding s__t and broke it.

I stepped up close to the mirror, stern faced and focused

Then I scrutinized my innermost ugly and took honest inventory of my broken

Just because my fathers weren't s__t doesn't mean I can't be better than both of them!

I reconciled and resolved issues with the damaged child within

And began an incredible transformation that allowed me to ascend

To heights that my wildest imagination couldn't even fathom

God blessed me with gifts that I'm still joyfully unraveling: a beautiful mind and an extremely creative pen

And I give Him all the glory.

He softened my heart, then opened my mind's eye and allowed me to rewrite my story

But most importantly, He instilled in me the ability to keep it real with me

He gave me the tools to repair my damage and connect all my dented dots

All this while I was alone with my thoughts.

I was a POPS Kid Before...

BY BOSTON WOODARD

I've been a POPS supporter since I first learned about it and had the privilege of writing the first article about POPS for the *Fresno Community Alliance*.

Amy Friedman and I regularly speak on the phone, and she once told me about the positive but sometimes emotional reactions people experience when hearing the students' stories. One POPS guest speaker had spent time in prison but had been free for many years when he came to speak to the students. As he spoke, tears welled in his eyes as he remembered himself at their age.

I wasn't surprised to hear that. When I began reading the first POPS Anthology, every piece I read brought me back to my years growing up in tumultuous family circumstances. Despite the chaos, the youth of POPS find ways to get up every day, go to school and stick with it, and I am inspired by their example.

Growing up on the back streets of Boston, my life was one huge hustle. I had no skills, no real friends, no education, no male role models, no clergy, no youth incentive program. There was nothing like POPS when I was growing up. As a juvenile everything I learned was instilled in me by criminals. I became a car thief at the age of twelve, and things escalated from there.

When my father went to jail, my mother was left with five kids to raise on her own. For years I didn't know where my father had gone, and we lived on welfare, with government cheese and canned goods for meals. New clothes came only at the start of the school year when my mother found a way to get us a pair of shoes and, when things were good, a new coat.

I ran away from home with no place in mind to go. Between the ages of 12 and 16, I slept in some of the coldest, nastiest, foulest-smelling places. In 1967, when I was 14, two friends and I stole some blankets from an abandoned trailer in Gloucester and made our way down to the waterfront where we broke into an abandoned warehouse, rolled out the blankets on the musty dirt floor. Waking up to the sound of seagulls screeching, the morning light revealed the truth: We had slept on ten inches of dried pigeon and sparrow crap. After that we slept in leaky, foul-smelling fishing boats. To this day I can smell the putrid stink of decomposing fish and diesel fuel.

The only people I felt comfortable around were the other kids who thought running away from broken families would fix everything. We became like brothers. And these days, in prison, I meet countless other prisoners who talk and think about their own pasts. I believe all incarcerated men and women parents should read the POPS anthologies; they'll remember their own pasts, and those who are parents will learn about what their children go through after they have gone to prison.

Many prisoners take full responsibility for their crimes. Many take measures while inside to break the cycle. Many sincerely want to change. One of the tools I use inside to judge others is to observe what they are doing when they think no one is watching, and truthfully, these days I see many men working hard to change their lives for the better. And many of my fellow prisoners tell me the POPS students are also inspiring them.

Because I believe so strongly in the principles of POPS the Club, I decided to something to help, so with the support of the administration at the California Medical Facility (CMF) state prison in Vacaville, on September 18, 2015, POPS the Club co-founders Amy Friedman and Dennis Danziger visited to speak to a crowd of 400 prisoners and staff, standing room only in CMF's Aaron J. Kuk Memorial Gymnasium. All the prisoners who attended the symposium were once POPS kids themselves or they have children out there now experiencing the pain of the prison system.

That day inspired another idea. Over the years I've been involved with many self-help and creative writing programs. When I learned there was no creative writing group available to the men at CMF, I solicited fellow prisoner and author Michael Davis to work with me to start the Creative Writing Guild inside CMF.

We wanted to create an atmosphere for our fellow prisoners to write, to read and to have our work critiqued. The Guild curriculum guides participants through a process, from brainstorming to drafting to revising and editing work. Our writers learn about different styles and resources, and receive encouragement and advice from instructors, classmates and handouts. CMF's Warden, Robert Fox and Chief Deputy Warden, D. Cueva, and Associate Warden, L. Bravo approved our application to start the guild to try something a little different inside.

Then we took it a step further.

We linked the Creative Writing Guild to POPS the Club. Thanks to CMF's administration, members of the Creative Writing Guild and men from the prison's general population are raising funds to donate to POPS the Club. Warden Fox and Chief Deputy Warden Cueva, prisoners, and staff at CMF are honored to be part of POPS the Club. Academic instructor Dave Hudson was instrumental in providing information and resources, helping our Guild to get off to a great start. CMF's administration has also approved a proposal that will allow guest speakers to visit our Guild.

We held one food sale and will continue to do so, and a portion of the money we raise goes to POPS the Club. I also hope other food sale eligible prisons throughout California will start programs like ours to support POPS.

After all, many of us were POPS kids before there was a POPS the Club.

BROKEN SILENCE

15 Years Gone

BY JAMEKA REYNOLDS

I never really open up about the subject of prison. I don't know how to put my words together to tell my story. I never knew there were people out there feeling the same pain I feel:

The pain of losing my father to the prison system at the age of 2 and being raised by a single mother of 3.

The pain of not getting to be daddy's little girl, and telling dad that boys are bullying me at school because I had short hair or I was too black.

The pain of seeing my mother struggle because daddy wasn't there.

The pain of my father seeing my first steps through prison glass and his not being there on my first day of school.

The pain of birthday cards in the mail instead of enjoying my father's presence on my special day.

I never really coped with the idea of my father being gone. I learned to live without him because I never really remember living a life with him.

Until now.

And 15 years of my life without him close by.

I didn't understand why it had to happen to me.

I didn't understand why I had to be the little black fatherless girl with the struggling mother.

I didn't understand, why me?

I've never really forgiven my father for leaving me. I've never really forgiven him for leaving me hanging without an explanation.

For leaving me hanging on Father-Daughter Dance Day while I danced with my mother; that wasn't her job!

I've never forgiven him for not being by my side when I cried myself to sleep from heartbreak because he wasn't here to tell me to stay away from boys.

I've never forgiven him for not even trying to be my father.

Prison took more than my father away from me.

When they took him away, they took my heart.

Now I'm stuck.

At 17 and trying to be daddy's little girl.

My Reinvigoration

BY MIREYA SANCHEZ ANNIBALI

I am a clock set on self-destruct
I am hidden, stuck behind walls to keep safe,
I am my greatest enemy,
I am the only person standing,
Yet, I am standing in my own way,
I am the finger looking to point and blame others for all my pain,
I am mad and upset,
I am lost and hidden and scared,
I am misunderstood and judged,
I am such a disappointment,
I am my worst judge.
But I am here,
And I am ready.

The Listener

BY GLORIOUS OWENS

All I do is listen
To the screams and shouts of the people I should care about most
But never feel sympathy towards.

All I do is listen
To people judging me for the way I dress.
"Why you always gotta dress like a boy?"

Or the things I do.
"Make sure you graduate and don't be a f--- up."

All I do is listen
Never speak up for myself.
What's the point?
Arguing only leads to louder arguing.

I'd rather use my fists.

What's the point in talking when no one is willing to listen?
They speak but never hear my words.
They judge, yet they haven't amounted to all that much.

But who am I to talk, right?

All I do is listen
To a mom who is never satisfied until I've broken down
To a sister who announces that she is grown but can barely
pay her bills
To a dad who always needs to know "Why this?" "Why that?"
To a brother who isn't around to hear the drama.
How happy he must be to have escaped the endless criticisms.

My head pounds,
Yet all I do is listen,
Absorbing all the negativity.

I wonder what the reasons are behind these hurtful words
Making a point?
Needing to be right?
The empty apology after seeing the pain that's been inflicted?

But all I do is listen
And I'm not sure why.

GLORIOUS OWENS
Portrait by Chris Wright

The Weapon Of Words

BY MELODY TREADWELL

My paper is the gun that holds the bullets of my ink shelled words. Each sentence triggers a gun shot to the reader's mind. Rupturing a thought that couldn't be put into words. Bleeding out emotions connected to the heart the reader is the victim of my deadly thoughts.

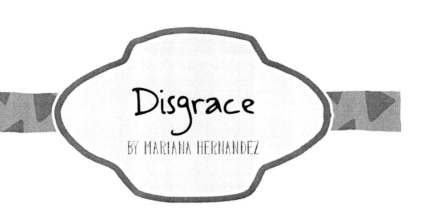

Disgrace

BY MARIANA HERNANDEZ

Most of us live in multiple worlds. I do too. My two worlds are my drug world and my church world. When you hear that, it doesn't sound well put together. It's hard having to deal with a good side yet knowing I have a bad side, too. I struggle with my two lifestyles. I try to maintain, but sometimes I break down because I feel like there will never be a resolution to the conflict. The two worlds don't mix well.

My drug world came upon me when I became a teenager. I have a sister who smokes weed every night, or most nights. My parents don't know. But since my freshman year in high school, I've adopted her habits.

Then there's my church world.

I walk into St. Augustine's Church every Sunday with my sister and praise the Lord. It's different walking into church, looking up to God, knowing I've sinned. He's seen it all. He's seen me smoke weed for the very first time. He's seen all my wrongs. On the other hand, I also worry not only about God but also the people I associate with at church—whether they are friends or just acquaintances. They all know me as the "young innocent girl." But nobody knows what I do or what

goes through my head every day. Sometimes I look to drugs, thinking they're a way out of my problems, that they'll help me erase all my bad thoughts. But it doesn't work.

It hurts looking at my parents, knowing what I've done—whether that was in the past or maybe in the near future, too. I truly don't know what's ahead for me. I feel disappointed in myself, but these things happen. I never understood how the priest in my church could read the words out of the Bible about humans sinning. We all do. Still, I know if the people in church and my family knew about my "sins" they would look at me differently from how they look at me now. I'm Catholic and I sin. What can I say? Nobody understands the hard life of living in two insane worlds. I'm not always going to be the innocent church girl. I say I can change.

I can't say I have resolved the problem. I still think about the tough situations from my drug-using past. But it's all in my head. It's called a past for a reason. I no longer physically use drugs, but I keep remembering and having flashbacks—definitely not something I like to picture. But I now know that I'll walk into church and may disagree with the fact of feeling that sinning is wrong, that it's a "disgrace," but that's how it is. I'll always be a Catholic. I'll continue to go to church every Sunday and I'll continue to avoid the drug world. It doesn't fit me any longer. I have friends who lead me in the right direction, friends who give me advice I value. Now I have priorities rather than addiction.

I know God will forgive me for my sins. I know I shall eventually get past my sins as everything passes along each road of my life.

Anxiety

BY HALEY ALVAREZ

It's when you feel
Helpless, breathless, empty

I've felt that

I've felt that to the point where
All I saw was black

Anxiety

It's when you feel like drowning in an
Ocean of all those kept feelings and
They try to swallow you whole like a
Whale swallows krill

I have been that teeny tiny krill

Anxiety has been the whale

My father's absence is my anxiety

Sorry for Saying Sorry

BY TYANNI GOMEZ

Sorry for being me.
Sorry for the mistakes.
Sorry for being a klutz.
Sorry for not being myself.
Sorry for the talk backs.
Sorry for not listening.
Sorry for not being perfect.
Sorry for being confused.
Sorry for being so quiet.
Sorry for being me.

I just think so much. You know that feeling when you just say, "I'm done," but you have to lift yourself up because you know you want to know more of your story and you just don't want to end so quickly? Or when you're in your room and you just sit there looking at cream walls in front of you and just think? You think about every single thing that has been bothering the living hell out of you. All because these problems you've been through haunt you. It's like your black shadow--it follows you even on your brightest days. Or when you still think and think and you get your hands and roughly grab your head and put them down asking yourself "why?" and you look around and that one tear drips down upon your eyes. Why does the past and present—and who knows, the future—bother me so much? I just want to know if I'm going to be okay because I'm 18 years old. My future is around the corner and I'm still lost. I'm still wondering if I can pick myself in the toughest situations because life is a b*tch on the most unexpected days.

Sorry about the past.
Sorry about the present.
Sorry about the future.
Sorry for being me.
Sorry.
Sorry for being sorry.

Are We the Same?

BY ANTHONY CORTEZ AND TYANNI GOMEZ

This story evolved out of a real text conversation between Venice High POPS the Club graduate Anthony Cortez and Tyanni Gomez, Venice High senior and POPS the Club President.

Tyanni wrote: I thought I "knew" him through his stories, but I never knew him. Every time he (in blue) messages me (in pink) back on this subject, I feel like I'm talking to myself. It's not bad. It's recovery. Are we the same? Not the story, but the way we feel. We wear a mask to not get asked.

Do you wear a mask?

> Yeah, right when I walk out of the house. What about you?

When I look into the mirror, I don't like what I see.

What is it that you don't like—
if I may ask?

I don't like what I see because I see all of my mistakes
and failures, people I have hurt and let down, I carry
this all in my head, I wear a mask so no one asks
what's wrong. I'm afraid I am on my own and no one
can relate.

Everyone has a mask. Everyone is afraid that
they are on their own. That's part of life. We take
responsibilities with the actions we take, but staying
in the past won't help. Accept the mistakes. Accept
the failures. People will get hurt or let down. Now I
know why I do too.

So why do you wear a mask—if I may ask?

My face changes right when I walk out the door
and when people see me they think, "Oh she's
always happy." Little do they know the ones that
smile hurt the most. It's more of the past when I'm
alone. I start to rethink every situation. I think the
worst question I hear throughout the day is, "How
are you?" because when I wear that mask, I lie.

I agree, the ones who seem most happy and giving to everyone else, over themselves, I believe are the ones who have seen pain and suffered. I am always thinking and over-thinking situations. Regret is my enemy. I hate the question "How are you?" Honestly I wish it never existed because sometimes I want to rant, let it all out, but I'm not going to waste anyone's time with my problems.

Overthinking is strange, as if you get controlled by it and it bothers the living hell out of you. We wish it never existed, and some others may feel that way too. "How are you?" are just three pathetic little words that make the person asking think they care.

I don't like when someone pretends they care when in reality they could care less.

We just wear a mask to not get asked.

BROTHERS & SISTERS

A Close Stranger

BY LUIS NUNEZ

When I was seven, I received a letter. My hands felt cold and numb as I opened the envelope. As I read the first line, my fingers shook.

"What's up, baby boy? My name is Ruben. I'm locked up in Lancaster State Prison over something that was not intended. Got racially profiled, misjudged and convicted. Nine years in the gutter. You're my blood and my brother. At this moment I know you're confused and conflicted."

My body grew heavy. I was clueless, stunned. I looked to my mom.

"Keep reading. You'll see."

Ruben told me to be strong and to always "stay blunt because life can get shallow, stressful and cold."

As I read on, I felt sad, bitter and distressed. Ruben had been robbed of his youth. He had no control over his life. And yet this letter that shocked and upset me also provided a dose of ecstasy. For I had found a new family member. Rather, a family member found me.

My brother Ruben and I began to correspond. I eagerly awaited each of his letters. Until one day, they stopped.

No more mail. No photos.

Two years later my mom planned a trip to search for her son, my brother.

When we arrived at the San Salvador airport in El Salvador, I saw my big brother for the first time. Of course, I instantly knew who he was.

He wore a black blazer, black slacks, black sunglasses, a white button up shirt and a slim back tie. He was really tall. He looked confident.

As I neared him he smiled and pulled off his sunglasses. He looked directly into my eyes and said, "Baby boy, it's me."

I froze. This was the first time I had seen my brother, this stranger. He grabbed me under my arms and lifted me up. My mother cried, spread her arms and hugged us both.

"Hey," he said, "we didn't meet to cry. Let's go have a vacation."

We spent the next few days splashing around at a water park and throwing ourselves into waves and building castles on the beach. At our hotel we hung out at the swimming pool racing each other in the pool and ordering pool side food service.

I felt as if my life was complete. I had somehow known, even at age seven, that there was something or someone missing from my mother's and my life, though no one had ever mentioned that I had a brother.

Ruben talked about his future plans and his past hurts.

We took long walks and made great memories together.

After a few days he drove us back to the airport and we said our good-byes.

I hugged him good-bye, though I didn't want to ever leave him, then turned, held my mother's hand, walked across the tarmac and up the steps to the plane. On the top step I turned and waved good-bye.

Ruben, sunglasses shielding his eyes, waved back.

I have not seen nor heard from my brother Ruben since.

On the Beach
Photograph by Juanito Hernandez

Sister

BY TYANNI GOMEZ

Life isn't that easy. My life consists of just plain depression. I guess when I'm happy, that's when sadness comes in and ruins the whole thing. Sucks ass. But what can I do? When I heard the news about my sister, I shattered, as if everything was gone and everything had turned into a nightmare. Maybe people suffer worse, but this is my worst. Maybe people have actually gone through this situation, but this isn't my sister. This isn't Ashley. Maybe there is worse news, but my news feels worse. I do have faith. I do because she's my sister and I love her so much, and I can't let her go—because she is the most beautiful human being I've met, she's my number one, she's my best friend, she's weird, she's funny, she always puts a smile on my face, but she is my sister, and God said, "Love one another," and God gave me that gift. To love and help the people who are in need, to have faith and hope that every little thing will be all right. Because God loves Ashley. God loves everyone, and I love her.

I Come from a Sister Who Doesn't Come Home

BY MARIANA HERNANDEZ

I come from a sister who doesn't come home at night. Who always smokes weed and reeks of alcohol.

I come from that unforgettable bitter scent that sticks to my skin.

Day by night.

Night by morning.

I wish it were different. I wish I could reverse the time and somehow take back all the bad habits that she's picked up.

Including the influences of her so-called friends.

For the past three years she's been addicted to drugs, mainly weed.

Things aren't the same with her anymore.

We no longer go to each other for advice or just to catch up.

There are things I've been dying to tell her, but I don't think she will understand where I'm coming from.

I can't rely on my big sister/best friend anymore.

I don't have her shoulder to cry on.

These small gestures meant so much to me; but now they feel like broken pieces that are unfixable.

It all changed so fast; and it feels as if I can do nothing to change her mind set on so many things.

I hope she finds herself along the way and finds her way back to our friendship.

I love my sister, but I also feel so much anger towards her. The positive emotions of a lifetime have begun to fade away.

I just want her back to her normal self.

I will always love her. I want her to know that.

I hope she does.

I Am An Only Child

BY DANIEL GONZALEZ

I am an only child.
I wonder how life would be if she was here.

I hear my mom crying on my shoulders.
I see the paramedics carrying her into the ambulance truck.
I want to know what actually happened.
I am an only child.

I pretend like nothing happened.
I feel like she's still with me.
I worry about my mom.
I cry with my mom when it's May 5th because my mom and
my sister have the same birthday.
I am an only child.
I understand that there's a moment we will die.
I ask why she had to go so fast.
I dream about her and have nightmares.
I try not to think about it, or else I cry.
I hope one day I will see her again.
I am an only child.

Losing My Brother

BY JOCELIN RUANO

From a young age, we all get educated about drugs and why we should stay away from them. I remember learning that marijuana was a gateway drug, but never did I think anyone I knew would move on to harder drugs.

When I was in the 4th grade, my older brother, sister, and I were sharing a room. I remember finding a bag of weed on my brother's dresser; pretending I didn't know what weed was or looked like at that time, I casually asked my sister "Hey, what is this?" to which she replied, "Oh it's trash." I remember her quickly rushing to my brother, and I overheard her tell him, "Next time your dumb ass decides to keep this in the house be smarter about where you leave it because Jocelin just found it!"

My brother eventually got caught high, and of course my parents said they would not tolerate it; obviously he didn't listen to them. Every time my brother was caught up, things got awful. My brother and dad would argue, leading to them physically fighting. My brother would often get kicked out or just simply leave the house. I remember him leaving once on the day of my birthday, around 3 a.m. I remember how much

I hated being away from my brother, so I began covering for him just so that he and my dad would not argue. As I got older, he began trusting me, so when I went out with my parents, he would text me to let him know when we were headed home so he could get the smell out of the house.

From all the covering and being there for my brother, we developed a great bond, a bond even my sister and I didn't have. My brother and I were like each other's other half. We liked the exact same foods, and it seemed like we had almost identical interests. Or was it just me following in my brother's footsteps? Whatever it was, never did I think about losing my brother.

A couple of years passed, he was still smoking, but now things had changed. Now he talked and laughed by himself. I'd ask him, "Haha dude, who are you talking to?" to which he responded, "Haha, no one, my imaginary friends since I don't have friends anymore." This seemed reasonable considering the fact that he had dropped all his friends for his ex-girlfriend.

Months after that, he was still talking and laughing by himself, except now he was getting violent. Now he was arguing as if someone were standing next to him. I started to worry. Was my brother going crazy? Was he okay? Should I inform someone about him? I remained quiet.

In July my brother was arrested for the first time. It wasn't a serious offense and things were still somewhat okay.

August of 2014 came, and my parents had to go out of town. My sister and my brother and I had the house to ourselves. My sister and I had plans for having friends over, but nothing went as planned. That night after dropping off my parents at LAX, my sister and I came home and fell asleep watching movies in the living room. We were awakened at 5 a.m. by my brother. He was turning on every light and opening all the doors claiming someone was trying to open his car. We told him we hadn't heard anything and there was no way because our gate was locked. My sister told him to calm down and get some sleep. She looked at me and said, "Oh my god, do you think Mom and Dad leaving was a bad idea?" I told her, "No, we'll be okay." But we weren't.

Every day that week just got worse and we couldn't even tell our parents because we didn't want them to worry. It got to the point that my brother didn't recognize us anymore, and he kept saying our family had all been killed. He began getting violent with us, and we had to call the police on him. The police took him to detox. The hospital called us to ask if we knew of the drugs he used, and we said we were only aware of him smoking weed but were sure he was using something else now.

The hospital called back and told us he had been using crystal meth. We were so shocked by the news, and of course we had to let our parents know. They were going to come home immediately, but both my sister and I knew they were on an important trip, so we told them we would handle it for the next week.

That week felt like a month. Our situation got so bad we couldn't stay in our house anymore because we were afraid he might hurt us. We were staying down the street with our aunt so that we could keep an eye on the house. We FaceTimed my parents daily, and we cried, wishing they were home already. Not a day went by that police weren't showing up at our house.

My parents finally came back from their trip, and things were somewhat okay. But that didn't last long. My brother started acting weird and violent again, not recognizing us once again. My parents were overwhelmed and didn't know what to do. They tried contacting different rehab centers but everyone said they would accept him only if he volunteered to come.

We held an intervention and asked him to please go, but he refused. I tried to be as strong as possible, for my mom. As strong as she is, I knew she couldn't handle this on her own, and my being down wasn't going to help her. I never let her see me cry. I poured my eyes out in the shower, and then I'd tell her everything would get better. "We're going to get him out of this together," I said to her.

Day by day things got worse, but my mom never lost hope. She had faith in God and always said, "God will listen to my prayers, He's the only one that can get my baby boy out of this." It hurt so much to see and feel the pain my mother was going through, but I kept it together.

Every night I'd lock myself up in my room and I cried and cried, and couldn't help but blame myself for my brother's addiction. I felt like I had done it to him by covering all those times he was smoking, and by not saying anything when I saw him talking to himself.

I didn't physically lose my brother, but mentally he was gone. What was the point of his physically being here if mentally he wasn't? The bond we had had was gone and that devastated me. I lost my other half, I lost the person who used to guide me on the right path, the only person I felt comfortable talking to. "I lost my brother," I said to myself every night as I cried myself to sleep.

Sammy Come Home

BY ROSIO SALAS

17. 17th birthday—and this is first time he's called me to wish me a happy birthday.

16. He called my mom and I answered. I let him know who it was. He said he had almost forgotten he had a little sister.

15. I don't know how he's doing or what he's up to, it can't be much, but I wish I knew something. Anything.

14. He did bad things again so of course he's back in jail.

13. I remember being awakened by the police who asked me question after question about him. "How is he at home?" "Is he violent?"

12. He was released from jail in 2011, but his freedom didn't last long.

11. His sentence was coming to an end. I still had no idea what he was like.

10.

9. It's been years of seeing my mom cry, seeing her fall apart and not being able to fix anything.

8. I remember waiting in long lines to go through security and then see him for what felt like 10 minutes. I've tried blocking out the feelings of it all, but the cold facility and those families who like us waited several hours just to hear the voice of their loved one will stay with me forever.

7. Cold folding chairs we'd sit on waiting to hear, "Visitation for Salas" and seeing my mom trying to keep it together for her little girl. That, too, will stay in my heart forever.

6.

5. My parents were always honest with me, always told me how things were and how bad he could be. I knew he'd be in for a while. I knew I had a brother who I hardly ever saw. I knew my parents were suffering.

4. My brother was a criminal and I knew it at a very young age.

PEOPLE WE LOVE

581 Letters

BY TYANNI GOMEZ

After school. Mom's car. Hi, Mom. We talk, laugh, argue. 405 Freeway down south. I hate you. Exiting off Carson Street. Left. Right on Acarus Avenue. Home. Open door. Hi Ashley. Hi Grandma. Hi Jordan. Okay, fridge. Orange juice. Yes. Walk out of the kitchen. Walk into my room.

I lock the door. I go into my bag. Take out my pen and notebook. I sit on the bed. I look towards the cream walls in front of me. I picture her in front of me. My grandmother, Leeta. She passed away in April 2014. I write to her every day since her passing. I wrote many letters telling her how my day was or how much I miss her. 83 weeks. 581 days. 13,944 hours. 836,640 minutes. 581 letters. Without her. I look down at my paper and write.

～

Dear Leeta,

The last time I saw you was October 2013, due to your leaving for Ecuador because Grandma Mirian couldn't take care of you. We didn't want to see you in pain, nor did I want to see you leave. It was hard. Very hard.

It's Monday. I just noticed my Youth Service Officers, my YSOs, are giving me a second chance to do a makeup test for Lieutenant this Saturday. I hope I pass. Oh, and my best friend is leaving for Mexico this week for a wedding. I'm going to miss her. I wrote again and again today in English. I love that class. I sometimes think you gave me this gift to release my emotions, so maybe I wouldn't be alone.

I miss you. Sometimes I wish I was with you. I miss you wearing that comfy white sweater of yours to the moment when I hugged you and felt your soft sweater, like a teddy bear. Or your delicious Sopa De Queso, I can taste the smell before you sweetly say...

"It's ready."

I sometimes wish I was with you, by your side, talking, laughing together in heaven. Even wondered what it was like up there.

Know that I will always appreciate every little thing you have done for me. Like folding my clothes, cooking for me, telling me it was going to be okay when I cried, watching Tom & Jerry together, giving me your kisses, and your oh-so-warm hugs.

Okay, Leeta. I gotta go. I'll write to you tomorrow.

With lots of love,
Tyanni

I'm tearing up while finishing the last sentence. A tear falls on my letter, again. I look up and whisper to myself, "Thank you."

And so...

Leeta taught me more than I could ever know. She taught me to care even more about people because one never knows what others are going through. She taught me to respect and be responsible for my actions. She taught me to express my emotions in writing. She taught me to be dedicated and motivated to whatever I want to achieve in life. Every time I lock that door in my room, I am myself. I'm home. I'm writing to her. 581 letters and many more to come. 83 weeks. 581 days. 13,944 hours. 836,640 minutes. 581letters. Without her.

TYANNI GOMEZ
Portrait by Doris Longman

Moving On
BY DANIEL GONZALEZ

He had a history. A history that he can never forget. Sometimes he wishes he could go back to that day to see what happened. He wishes he could time travel to save Elky from drowning alongside his Uncle David. She died at age two. He was only eight when it happened.

He had more problems though. He heard arguments at six every evening. A daily affair. His dad came home drunk, trying to forget what happened to his daughter. Now school wasn't the same for him. He didn't want to go anymore. His friends would talk to him but he only longed to be alone. At home he just entered his room and lay down, looking up at the ceiling and watching the dark shadows move. He imagined his sister was there with him.

He had one meaningful thing though. Sometimes that took his mind off everything else. Soccer became his best friend. Soccer was there whenever he needed help. Therapy didn't help. Sitting across from the lady in a quiet room answering questions or playing checkers didn't help. It was a soccer ball. Yes, just a soccer ball that helped him move on. Yet his sister will always be in my heart.

First Meet

BY ANGELA HERNANDEZ

I can hear my heart beating.
I can hear myself laughing at his jokes.
I can smell the curly fries from Jack in the Box as we walk to my house.
I can feel our hands shaking as if we were very nervous.
Oh wait…we are.
It's the first time he's coming over for dinner with my family.
I open the gate to my house, slowly and lead him in.
As I slam the gate, leaves fall down from the tree as if like snow; but sadly, it doesn't snow in L.A.
We stop and turn to each other when we arrive at my door.
I can hear my breathing.
I can feel him shaking.
I look into his eyes and say to him, "Ready?"
From where we're standing I can hear them laughing from the other side of the door.
I squeeze his hand and he squeezes mine.
I open the door, as I walk in first
I smell the sweet apples that are in the basket beside the entrance.
And it started with a "hello."

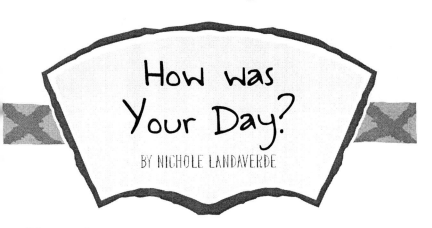

How was Your Day?

BY NICHOLE LANDAVERDE

February 6

NOT SO HAPPY NOTE:

I visited the happiest person today. He didn't look so good. He wasn't happy. He was bald. He was attached to a rolling-rack looking thing. He couldn't eat solids. He had a backpack that hung on the rolling-rack, where he received his foods and vitamins. I tried so hard to keep a smile on because we used to get along so well. He would visit my family when my mom passed away. He talked with me when it hit me the hardest. He is the person that can talk me out of my sad moments. I want to be around him more than I am now but he lives in Fontana, two hours away. I know he will get better but I wouldn't wait until then to be optimistic. "Cancer doesn't kill you, it's your bad reaction that does," his wife said. She was the happy one. Well, she kind of has to be.

HAPPY NOTE:

I love going to Fontana. I love the joy it brings me to visit my uncle's side of the family. The Mexican pride they have is contagious. Any little thing is a party to them—baby showers, weddings, birthdays, etc. I visited a baby shower that was hosted at a nearby park. All gatherings take place there. I don't visit often but that is due to the distance. I was extremely excited to go this time because I was looking forward to visiting my favorite person as well.

The Journal

BY JOSE PINA

A Friday in third grade.

Back then I didn't like school. Hated reading and writing. I went to school to hang out with friends.

On this one Friday, my teacher, Mrs. Gutierrez, told me to stay in at lunch.

I figured I was in trouble. That happened now and then. But now I felt confused.

She dismissed everyone else in class to lunch.

When everyone else was gone, she shut the door. Told me to sit.

She handed me a journal and this is exactly what she said, "Jose, whenever you are mad or happy write in this journal. It'll help."

I knew I would not write one word in it, but I grabbed the book anyway.

Every morning thereafter as I dressed for school I would always see the journal resting untouched on my bedside table.

Weeks passed and I hadn't cracked its cover.

One day I received some horrible news.

My grandpa passed away.

Heart attack.

I didn't know what to do; what to say; how to act.

My thoughts flew everywhere.

I felt lost, negative, angry.

I missed school the next four days.

On the fifth morning after my grandpa passed, I woke staring straight at the journal.

I debated whether or not to record my thoughts as Mrs. Gutierrez had told me.

At first it felt weird, writing. Because I always hated writing.

But for the next 90 minutes, no-stop, I wrote.

And for the first time since my loss I felt a sense of peace within me.

The following day I returned to school filled with hope and courage.

The moment I stepped into Mrs. Gutierrez's classroom I thanked her. I told her that she changed the way I looked at things, felt about the world.

Since that morning of endless writing I've written every day, regardless of whether I was up or down. Didn't matter. I wrote.

Writing gave me structure and made me realize that wasting my time in school was a losing proposition.

To this day I cherish Mrs. Gutierrez. I don't know how I would have made it through that difficult time had it not been for her gift of all those blank pages.

Now I love writing and I see myself writing and writing for decades to come.

Ella Se Fue

BY LESLIE MATEOS

She is gone

"I still remember when I left you, now I know that I made the wrong decision, the tears I cry are from pain. Everything was a huge mistake. Why did I leave you?"

There's nothing sadder than an empty house. The woman he loves is now gone because of him. Now he misses her company and the loving things she would say, to which he never corresponded. He was blind, he treated her badly and for a while cheated on her with another woman. He didn't care about her love, and now he is dying from the pain.

She was like a flower that dried up because it was never watered. It slowly started dying and he never even noticed. He hopes that one day his tears will help her sprout again. He understands her reasons for leaving and hopes that one day she'll forgive him. He was the one that pushed her away, so there is no reason for him to complain. The only thing he can keep are the memories.

Talking to his pillow at night, he remembers her touch, her eyes, the scent of her body, and the figure of her hair. He didn't want to lose her. That was his fear. He knows it was his fault, he treated her badly.

Broken Pieces

BY KATHERINE SECAIDA

I don't want to worry any more.
I don't want to waste any more time.

I always found a way to love you, even after all you put me
through,
Your lies and games.
I wish we were on the same page,
But deep down I know we never will be
I just like to think that we are.

I get aggravated over things that happened in the past,
But you never see your mistakes, D.
I panic, hoping you won't lie to me again, but that's all you do.
I said something to you. I was mad.
I wanted you to realize what you were doing to me
So I dropped down to your level.
That was wrong of me.

I always worried you were doing things behind my back
While I was at home wondering what was going on.
You left me for seven months and came back on New Year's
Eve, at a party.

I questioned everything.
I wondered: *Why do I still love you?*

I pulled the blankets over my body
as you got in bed and wrapped your arms around me saying,
"Please stop,"
I pushed you off.
You didn't give up.
You just wrapped your arms around me and whispered in my
ear,
"I'm sorry Katherine, I didn't mean to upset you."
I said, "I just want the best for you."

For those seven months we weren't together, I thought about
you.
I cried myself to sleep.
I thought about the times we shared, our laughter and tears.
I knew deep down inside you cared, you love me,
But you never show it until I'm gone.

Once we were doing homework.
I lay down on my stomach, feeling the soft blue carpeting
against my body
I held my black binder and worksheets.
I guess you were staring at me.
You got off your bed, fell to the ground, wrapped your cold,
bare hands around my warm body and hugged me as tightly
as you could,
And in seconds you fell asleep.
I pretended everything was okay
But all I wanted to do was cry.

I've done that.
I remember crying over your bare body,
Repeating the words: "You left me for seven months,
Why do you keep leaving and coming back?"
You pulled me closer and told me over and over that you
loved me.

I can tell you're broken, and I know why.
I've used your problems against you
And I can't take those words back.
But I've tried everything.
I gave you my body, my heart, my mind,
What else do you want?

You always made sure I was safe
But sometimes I felt you didn't care.
I wish I knew what this year would bring.
I want to know why you keep coming back into my life?
What is the purpose?

You know how to pull me back.
I know how to break you.
You told me that I was the first girl who ever said such harsh
things.
I can tell you: You're the first boy I ever gave my all.

March 9, 2016 is the last day you'll ever hear from me.
I'm tired of the tears running down my face.
It's time to let go of you.
This time I ended it.
Here I am picking up your broken pieces
Putting them back together.

You never helped me, but that's okay.
When you finally realize I loved you
And I got under your skin for a reason
You'll do something better for yourself.
Then you'll come back with no broken pieces.

This isn't my loss.
This is yours.
I'll be fine.

LINDA DURAN
Portrait by Chris Wright

HOW WE LIVE

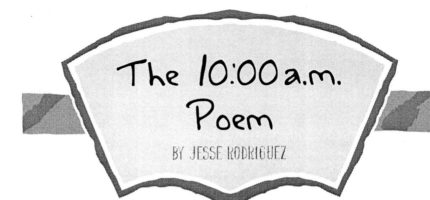

The 10:00 a.m. Poem

BY JESSE RODRIGUEZ

Sunny day, roses bloom
Two more hours until it hits noon
Light beaming, dogs barking
Blue sky, day starting
Students running, buses stopping
Stomp the yard, bags dropping
Teachers screaming
Students dreaming
The day's rolling
Feels slow it's still morning
On social media, all just scrolling
We all wanna have fun, just go bowling.

Memories

BY MARIA GARCIA

She had a history. Her life wasn't as perfect as people thought it to be but her life wasn't hell either. She was eight when she first went to Disneyland, excited to see her favorite princess, Snow White, and excited to get on the rides. She was happy to be in the Happiest Place on Earth, what kid wouldn't be? Every Sunday after church she and her family would go to Plaza Mexico. They would eat, go around stores buying point-less stuff and sometimes staying to watch the Mariachis play. After all they had a blast, they did everything as a family. But her brothers grew older and dedicated all their time to their girlfriends. Her father's paycheck was getting low and the bills were getting high, and soon her mother found a job and all the adventures they had had as a family were history.

Her life wasn't sad but it was boring. To pass the time she would hang out with her friends. It was always jokes and laughs, risks and dares. Long conversations on the rooftop where they felt the late night mist and saw the dull, gray moon and wished upon a star. Talked about their goals, fears, what they would do if they became president. She never felt alone when she was with friends, but once she opened the door to her silent home, she felt lonely. She took long walks around the park. She still had hope that her family would go back to being a happy family. After all, she was still growing, and the future would soon become history.

pretEnd

BY KOBE TOMAS

I pretend life's perfect
Always puffing pot
In my parking lot
I swear when I think life ain't fair
I don't really cry, when I die
I don't want anyone to cry

Waking up every morning not knowing
if ima live or die today
Coming out my pad bumping
Live or die in LA
I live in the present 'cause it's a gift to be appreciated
Because suicide is so overrated
From rope hugs to heavy drugs
I understand and I know god has a plan
For everybody nice or naughty

No Justice

BY PARADYSE OAKLEY

There's a burden on my chest every day
I'm waking up
My dad's incarcerated
That's a struggle every day
But I must strive to succeed
Both in track & life—with education.
Some days I don't want to get up
But then I remember the letters you write me
I must set an example for Parys & Lacey.
So I reach for the limit
Hoping that I don't let anyone down on the way.
Some days I don't want to get up
Because I know all the injustice that's
Going on all across the world
People dying for no reason
Others trying to cover up
Hands up, don't shoot!
But "don't care," fire anyway
Five or forty shells dropping to the floor.
Now we are marching and protesting.
No Justice No Peace
We have little kids dying.
For what?

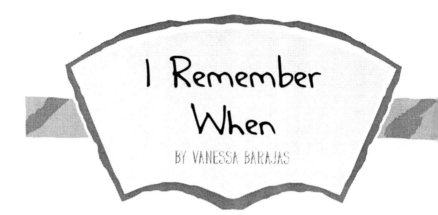

I Remember When

BY VANESSA BARAJAS

I remember when I had the time to spend time with friends and never dealt with problems of any sort.

I remember when I was in elementary school, I loved spending time alone on the soccer field at school, society never judged a kid wanting to be alone at times, it was different.

I remember when I had my best friend beside me, waiting for the future.

Sadly, I remember when I never spoke to my best friend anymore.

I remember when my mind and actions changed because I had ideas of how to act like everyone else, being normal.

I remember when I graduated eighth grade and I knew that I'd never see my good friends anymore.

I remember when I entered high school as a freshman. Being alone there was scary. I didn't know anybody.

I remember when I met my first group of friends. They welcomed me.

I remember when I was a sophomore, I signed up for drumline. I was joining without knowing how to read music.

I remember my first football game, it was my first time performing a cadence as a bass player. I couldn't settle my nervous self to readiness. It was fun though.

I remember when I always went to watch movies at the theaters with my movie buddies, waiting to see the previews to plan future Saturday nights out.

I remember when my senior bandmates graduated, which sucked, they taught me how read music and play.

I remember when the first weeks as a junior, friends found their way on their own. I did too, with all the stress of academic pressure and tutoring.

I remember how much I procrastinated during all my years in school.

I need to remember for future use to keep up and not worry about what's ahead of me.

Open Minded and Loud

BY DAISY LOPEZ

I am Daisy Lopez
I am 16 years old
I am the youngest out of four
I am the craziest
I am strong
I am forgiving
I am trustworthy
I am the one with the fake smile
I am the one who pretends that everything is fine but really it isn't
I haven't lived a crazy life, but I have lived in a pretty messed up one.

I am open minded and loud
I wonder what people think of me
I hear nonsense here and there
I see different sides of others
I want people to understand what my life consists of
I am open minded and loud.

I pretend that I'm the happiest, most joyful young lady
I feel like a bird that can't seem to fly
But lifts its wings and keeps trying to show others that not being able to fly
Doesn't mean they are nothing in life.
I worry about violence
I cry for the world
I am open minded and loud

I can't quite understand this world
I say there should be peace and love
I dream of looking up to the stars and finding a miracle
I try to do my best
I hope that one day people will understand where I come from
I am open minded and loud.

"happy thanksgiving"

I MISS THE TURKEY

THANKSGIVING WAS MY FAVORITE TIME OF YEAR
COOKING AND EATING TOGETHER AS FAMILY SHOULD..
THEN YEARS PASSED AND THE TABLE BECAME EMPTY
MY DAD DISAPPEARED, MY UNCLE IS cusmi AWAY IN MIAMI,
MY COUSIN HAS FLED, AND MY AUNT IS GONE.
EVERY YEAR PASSES BY AND IT'S NOT THE SAME
FAMILY WAS EVERYTHING AND
THANKSGIVING WAS MY FAVORITE HOLIDAY.

MONA VIERA
11-12-15
P. 4

Point of View

BY JESSE RODRIGUEZ

Money come money go
Follow the rhythm go with the flow
High school come mindsets change
Don't you find that kinda strange?
Every day we make new friends
Perfect start, but there's the end
To get to the top, it's 'bout respect
If you don't give that then what you expect?
As day play its role, bullets fly
Yellow tape, families cry
We have million dollar players
Why can't we have a single dollar prayer
Innocent people having cancer
But we question God 'cause we know he has the answer
People drink and smoke to heal the pain
It's like asking the sun to bring no rain
We are all unchained slaves
Beaten 'til bare bones but we have to be brave
We try and expect the best but at times get the worst
Poor kids hungry and dying of thirst

COUNTDOWN

9 Years of Darkness

BY MAYNOR GALLETAN

18. My father has moved prisons and I have no idea where he is.

17. Decide to write my father a letter and I accidentally made him worry.

16. My dad calls my aunt's phone because he thinks my mom gets mad when he calls.

15. I write my dad once in a while.

14. I write my dad all the time, create drafts to make sure what he gets is perfect.

13. Girls are interesting but I haven't been taught what to do.

12. Mom still loves dad but wonders if she should move on.

10. Visit my dad in a San Bernardino prison weekly.

9. I haven't seen my dad in a year.

8. Dads rushing out of the house, I find out later he was trying to run from the police.

7. My favorite car is my dad's 2 door convertible, leather interior, mustang.

6. I go everywhere with my dad.

5. I have 2 mini bikes (red & blue).

4. Disneyland bores me because I go there every weekend.

3. Dad shows me off because I'm much better looking than most 3 year olds.

2. I already have jewelry on.

1. My face is stuffed with milk every time I cry because he doesn't know what else to do.

0. My dad is happy to begin his family, even more ecstatic.

XVII

BY IONA SCOTT

XVII: I've thought of inviting my mom to my graduation.

XVI: I got into an argument with my stepmom; we stopped talking even though we live in the same house.

XV: Found out my cousin on my mom's side was pregnant at 15. Before I moved back to California, we made a promise to break the chain.

XIV: My Aunt Laurie, from my dad's side, fought diabetes for as long as I could remember. After four years of being away, she called in, but I didn't speak to her. A few months later she passed away.

XIII: The first year since I moved back to California from Rhode Island, and I no longer speak to my mom.

XII: I got kicked out of my first school since being back in California.

XI My dad won the custody case, primarily because my mom didn't show up to court to hear the decision.

X: I moved back east with my mom. I found out my Uncle Johnny had sold drugs out of his house since before I was born. He just had his third kid.

IX: We were living out of hotels before we finally moved into an apartment, first time I'd been to California.

VIII: My grandma, from dad's side, offered to let me live with her. My mom said no because she thought my grandma would keep me from her.

VII: My Aunt Elsa, from my mom's side, was diagnosed with cancer. The third person in my mom's family.

VI: My dad made the final decision to move out and leave my mom. They hadn't been on good terms in years.

V: My grandpa, from Dad's side, offered my parents one of his homes. My dad turned down the offer because my mom said no, for no apparent reason.

IV: My mom was diagnosed with kidney stones, and years before that cancer. She was the second one to get cancer.

III: My Aunt Luisa, on my mom's side, was diagnosed with cancer. She was the first.

II: I lived with my grandparents from dad's side 99% of the time while my parents tried to figure things out.

I: Dad finally got my mom to stop living with her sister. He helped her move out.

0:   Mom was told she couldn't have kids. I was born May 20, 1998.

Life's Ups and Downs

BY COLBIE WITHERSPOON

17. I was accepted into Cal State University Dominguez Hills

16. I was put into therapy due to my nervous breakdown

15. I completed a 26-mile hike through the woods to the highest mountain in Southern California

14. I had my very first Disneyland experience

13. I got drunk for the very first time and passed out

12. I threw a chair across the classroom due to being bullied all the time in class

11. I lost a good friend to a car accident

10. I culminated from fifth grade

9. My grandmother passed away from Diabetes

8. I was about to flunk out of third grade

7. My father was taken to prison

6. My cousin was sentenced to 50 years in prison for drug dealing

5. I have my first birthday party with all my friends

4. My dad left me at home alone to go see my stepmother

3. My dad told me he loved me and would never leave me

2. I said my first few words

1. My mom told me that I was the best thing that had ever happened to her

0. On 8-8-1998 12:45 p.m. I was born into this life

At 15

BY LILLIANA GARCIA

15. Everything between my dad and me has changed for the worse. He's gone from spending a lot of time with me to barely even calling me.

14. Mom starts doing more for me. Like paying for the roof over our heads and paying all the bills.

13. Dad slowly stops paying attention to me.

12. Not daddy's little girl anymore. Now he has a kid with his new girlfriend. It hurts because I receive so little attention from him.

11. I say to myself, "Why is he giving her more attention than me? I'm his daughter!"

10. Feel kicked to the curb when dad brought his girlfriend into his life. Into my life, too.

9. I carry a backpack around because I stay with dad every other weekend. Feel like a traveling salesperson.

8. Dad starts paying child support.

7. Mom and dad separate.

6. I wake up most mornings to the sounds of my parents arguing over who is going to watch me.

5. Always want to be with my dad. I'm his only child and he will buy me anything I want.

4. Dad teaches me to play softball.

3. I start to be daddy's little girl. I love it.

2. Mom leaves it up to dad to see who is going to watch over me for the day.

1. I am carried around all the time. Feel loved.

0. I enter the world.

As The Years Go By

BY EMIRIA HENRY

16. Finally quiet in the house. It's not home, Dad would have to be there for that. Momma's happy though. Good for her.

15. My mom gets tired of yelling all the time. She tells my dad to go and not to come back. He cries…of course he does.

14. New school. No familiar faces. I wish my mom knew what I went through in a day. I stay strong for her, not him.

13. I don't feel any better. Everything's supposed to be different but it isn't. When do I get to be happy?

12. I wake up scared. Daddy's stumbling into the house. Momma cries and screams. She's not the scary one.

11. Daddy doesn't have to work as much. I love him so much.

10. I have a best friend now. She promised she'll be here for me.

 9. Am I a burden to them?

 8. Still can't breathe. No one needs to know.

 7. My sister's happy. She gets to go to high school. That seems fun. She won't have to be here.

 6. Daddy had an accident. Mommy says he's fine. I guess…

5. Mommy tells me to go back to sleep, but I can't. Daddy won't let me.

4. I'm not supposed to be up this late, but Daddy's too loud. He won't tell his friends to leave. Mommy doesn't say anything.

3. I don't see Daddy as much but I know he loves me. Even with the new addition to the family. Love you, baby brother.

2.

1. I can't breathe…

0. I open my eyes for the first time and smile. She's beautiful.

THINKING…

Photograph by Juanito Hernandez

What's Dad?

BY ROSA ISELA RUIZ

17. Almost turning eighteen and still don't know who my father is.

16. Asking myself if my father would accept my sister and me, also if he is alive.

15. Asking my mother for the third time: Who is my father?

14. My sister doesn't want to know anything about our father.

13. It's sad how I see my cousins and friends who have fathers, and I don't.

12. Sad not knowing who my father is.

11. First time asking mother who is my father?

10. Not knowing why my father is not with me.

9. Teachers asking who my father is or where he is. No answer from me.

8. Been bullied for not having a father.

7. Your own family discriminates against you for not having a father.

6. My father is my grandpa; he was there when I was born.

5. Having a stepfather.

4. First day of school, men are arriving with little girls. What's dad?

3. Don't know what the word Father means.

2. Dad didn't watch my first steps.

1. I cry, only Mom comforts me.

0. Little did Mom know she was having twins. Little did Dad know we exist.

Life Backwards

BY ELSA RAMIREZ

17. My mom is in the process of adopting my nephew

16. My sister can no longer raise her son.

15. My mom has custody of my nephew. I'm glad he's back home.

14. It's November 6, 2012, my birthday. I come out and find out my nephew was taken away by social services.

13. My sister is no longer the same. She yells at me for no reason. My friend told me she saw her hit the pookie pipe, but I have no idea what that is.

12. My mom has an anxiety attack due to the fact that my sister went to jail last night for threatening a cop.

11. It's 3 a.m. I can't sleep. I hear the phone ring constantly. I go to my dad's room to see what's up. He tells me my 18-year-old sister was in a bad car accident. She's in a coma and they don't know whether she'll live or not.

10.

9. I'm sleeping on the couch. My ears are wide open to the yelling upstairs. I hear my 16-year-old sister tell my mom she's pregnant.

8. I am pulled out of school. I'm not sure why. We're at Venice High and it turns out my sister is getting expelled for carrying a knife in her bag.

7. I'm at church with my whole family. Everyone is at the altar getting prayed for. The preacher tells my mom to be careful with my sister. A lot of bad things will come her way if she doesn't follow God's path, he says.

6.

5.

4.

3.

2.

1.

WHERE WE ARE FROM

I Come from Gospel Music Blasting at 4 a.m.

BY GLORIOUS OWENS

I come from gospel music blasting at 4 a.m.
from my mom speaking in tongues praying for a better life
for her kids

I come from snitches get stitches
and I was the main one beaten

I come from hearing gunshots on Century and Hoover
right outside my house
and pressing my face against the tiles
to hold my little sisters to keep them from crying

I come from never letting anybody take my lunch money
and beating down the bullies
to always being in the principal's office
for slapping a kid in class

I come from sports being my only outlet
for the anger I feel for my enemies

I come from staying at my friend's house after volleyball games
because it's too dark to catch the train alone in the hood

I come from feeling like a burden
for being too loud at school and too quiet at home

I come from acting tough in front of other people,
but being scared and childish in front of my family

I come from South Central.

I Remember

BY ROSA MARIA RUIZ

I remember when I was five years old, my sister and I had to move to Oaxaca with our grandparents. My mom had to go to the U.S.A to make money for her two daughters.

I remember not having my mother for my sixth, seventh, eighth, ninth and tenth birthday. She was working so hard for us to have nice birthdays with our grandparents.

I remember throwing myself in a river in Oaxaca so I could learn how to swim. That's the way I learned how to swim in the hard-court.

I remember never asking my mother who my father was, because my mom never had a portrait of him. I never had imagined how he looked, because I knew that my grandpa was my father.

I remember when my grandma taught me to wash the dishes. Also she taught me how to make handmade tortillas and delicious salsas and guacamole.

I remember when I was seven years old. I threw a rock to my sister's forehead because I got jealous of her. My mom was hugging her too much. Good thing it wasn't something big like opening her forehead, because my mom wouldn't have forgiven me.

I remember when our first dog died. We were in the river washing our clothes. My grandma tied her next to an oven were my grandpa used to make brick and she died hanged. When I went to hang my clothes to a rope, I didn't hear my dog at all I went to check on her. She was dead already.

I remember when my grandmother used to cook the reindeer and armadillo and make some stew. My grandma used to make tamales of iguana. She also used to make a salsa of ants. We used to eat turtle eggs by themselves. I miss my grandmother, but right now I like to eat my moms tamales. If you like to go and eat wild animals, I recommend you to go to Oaxaca.

ROSA MARIA RUIZ
Portrait by Chris Wright

I Come From

BY KOBE TOMAS

I come from the ghetto, born and raised in this hell hole.
Where the raspado man is like a Baskin Robbin's ice cream stand.
I come from the block where I learn to walk and run from cops
I come from my father's sand
I mean the Mother Land.
I come from convicts and addicts and still don't have any family pics.
I come from bumming brew on the corner to becoming an everyday stoner.
I come from different ghettos, from Koreatown to South Central to Pico-Union.
I come from a hard working mother and no father figure
I come from tags, throwies, and bombs
I come from a broken home where I always feel alone that's why I'm always out and about
I'm trapped in the ghetto and it feels like I'm locked inside my own pad.
I don't know how to get out.
But I know I will
it's easy to know where you come from but
it's hard to figure out where you're going.

193

Hadn't Expected That

BY ELSA RAMIREZ

It's sixth period. I'm sitting, thinking about life, waiting for the 15 minutes of silent reading to finally end.

"All right, everyone take out paper and something to write with, we're going to do some simple warm up exercises," Mr. Danziger says.

I dig into my bag, grab a sheet of paper and a pencil.

"I want you guys to write about where you come from," he says.

"You know what?" I tell myself, "I'll just do this later."

Fact is, I know exactly where I come from, yet nothing comes to mind.

When I arrive home, I turn on my computer. I sit, think. Nothing happens. This is new. I've rarely had trouble writing.

I start to think about the people who live in my neighborhood.

Finally, I begin to write. About my lifestyle. About the lives of people around me. About what I see and would rather not see.

The next day I enter Mr. Danziger's class, hand him my paper, sit.

It's silent reading again. And I'm daydreaming again.

But then I hear myself say, "You know, maybe I'll read out loud this time."

I do.

But I'm interrupted.

"Elsa, can you meet me out in the hallway for a second?" Mr. Danziger asks.

"Oh f- ! What did I do this time?" I think.

I walk into the hallway; my heart is pounding. I'm scared.

"Elsa," he says, "your I Come From piece is incredible writing."

I am shocked. I honestly thought it wasn't all that good.

"Oh, wow, thank you!"

"I was wondering if we can publish it in this year's POPS anthology?"

"Of course you can."

"Great. I'll need you to sign the release papers."

"Okay."

I return to class feeling proud of myself. I hadn't expected that.

After that, I started attending POPS the Club meetings on a regular basis.

As I continue to attend I am more and more inspired to write. And to become a better writer.

This is my piece:

I COME FROM WHERE VIOLENCE IS THE ANSWER TO EVERYTHING

I come from a neighborhood where violence is the answer to everything

I come from where being a project kid is a lifestyle

I come from where girls get pregnant and their baby daddies get locked up in jail

I come from a hood where no one wants to see you do better

I come from where loyalty is questioned because the people who were so-called friends backstab you

I come from where gunshots become music to one's ears

I come from parents who don't care what I do because they are tried from chasing my sisters out in the streets

I come from not eating if the food stamps don't arrive

I come from where the struggle is real

I come from being the first one in my family who will go to college

Nothing Is Wrong

BY YESENIA GOMEZ

I come from a place where police officers, social workers, detectives, and living with other families is natural. I come from only being able to see my family every other weekend.

I come from starving because my foster mom wouldn't feed me.

I come from being locked in my room because I wasn't family.

I come from being moved from school to school because my foster parents didn't like me.

I come from a dad who would drink and smoke but stopped when my mom got pregnant.

I come from a dad who was accused of sexual abuse.

I come from a mom who sold drugs.

I come from a dark past that I think maybe no one understands

I come from faking a smile because I am great and nothing is wrong.

I Wish

BY VANESSA BARAJAS

I wish...

I wish I could change the world today.

I wish I could feel more than today's freedom.

I wish the beginnings of the industrial era had never spread around the world.

I wish everyone had a clear mind about who is the enemy, the sickness, and who is the friend, the cure.

I wish that before the creation of government, slavery, industrialization or wars, people had started thinking carefully about their future.

I wish the way we eat and produce food had been from clean farmland, not from factories.

I wish technology was for discovering a cure.

I wish that everyone could look at one another without one single criticism.

I wish that money was no longer the big problem.

I wish that Mother Nature's creatures were not in danger of permanent extinction.

I wish that everyone had faith in one another.

I wish there had never been a single war.

I wish all city space and army bases were put to better use.

I wish I could go back in time and see what went wrong.

I Come from a Place I Once Didn't Know

BY VALERIA DELA TORRE

I come from a place I once didn't know
The place I was born, down south across the border
One day I asked my mom when we could go visit
She said, "There's no way back after."

I come from 1.4% of K-12 undocumented students
Who want to pursue the American Dream
I come from every teardrop
I've seen roll down my mother's cheek
Because the vision of that dream
isn't always bright

I come from a country I don't know
but wish to one day
go back and meet

WHERE WE STAY

I Come From

BY BIANCA LOPEZ

I come from hell behind a brown wooden door.
Where I hear yelling and crying at 8 in the morning.
I come from where a mother would kick out her own
daughters over a dog,
Where she thinks it's okay to ignore us and bitch at us and
let go of her daughters.
I come from a father never caring for us or supporting us,
Where we can't even talk to him because he starts saying
that we bug him too much and just yells.
I come from a place where both parents give up on their kids,
Where I can't ask for their help with anything because I
know they won't help.
I come from a mother telling her daughter to not even ask
for any help because she won't.
Where I'm struggling and crying and feel like I'm trapped in
a box, but Mom she still won't help me out.
I come from parents who are willing to give up and kick us
out.

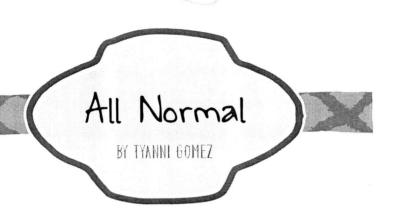

All Normal

BY TYANNI GOMEZ

It was all normal to me.
Culver City Projects or the nice way, "Mar Vista Gardens."
Boom.
Did you hear that? Someone got shot. Again.
Boom Boom.
Oh don't worry. It's just fireworks.

I always looked out the window, but carefully. I crawled out of my bed and opened the curtains very gently. No view of anything or anyone. Must've been at the other side of the projects.

Throughout my years in the projects. If you had loud music, you just had loud music. You were a savage if you called the police about the loud music. I mean people would raise the volume like crazy so that you could hear it eight buildings down (that's a long way).

Throughout my years in the projects. If you heard gun-shots, they didn't concern. Gunshots were normal. I slept to the noise of the boom. Nothing new. I mean my next door neighbor shot herself in the house because she believed she couldn't do anything worthwhile. She left her one-year-old kid. No parents.

Throughout my years in the projects. If you heard an argument outside or next door, you let them be. You didn't interrupt them because then they would continue—to the point of having a cat fight. Sister to sister. Yeah, I saw it all. Like I said, open the curtains very gently. I mean the girls yelled like crazy, louder than the PE coaches telling you to finish up that last lap.

Throughout my years in the projects. I wasn't allowed to go outside much. Mom said it was too dangerous, but I didn't believe that. Because it was so normal to me I wasn't afraid, to the point when my best friend played Barbie with me at the window. I was inside and she was out.

Throughout my years in the projects. I saw people get arrested. Maybe around 30 or more. My mom and I would just look through the window. We had this silence in ourselves, we weren't surprised or anything. We were just tired of seeing this every day, if not in the morning then at night. If not night, afternoon.

Throughout my years in the projects. I saw maybe 3 dead bodies. My first one was when I was around 6 or 7 years old. But it was from a distance. Someone got shot. My mom picked me up from school. We walked home and then my mom stopped and squinted. I looked at her first, then looked where she was looking. She just said...

"Someone died."

I just stayed silent and we both walked.

Throughout my years in the projects. This girl wanted to hit me because she just didn't like me. She was about 14 years old and I was 7. She hated me with a passion. I didn't care nor was I scared. She said, "Just see, watch."

I looked down at my Barbie watch and looked up to her and said...

"Well, 5:18 p.m., and you're not doing anything."

She never touched me after that.

Throughout my years in the projects. You either saw drugs or people smoking, high as a kite, and there were deals here and there at the park or at my neighbor's house. One door down from me on the right side. People even came out at 3 in the morning just to get drugs, with one simple whistle.

Throughout my years in the projects. I found everything normal. My mom put me in a DAPS Program. A program for kids 9 to 12 to learn basic things about law enforcement and leadership skills. I've walked into detectives' offices, run into officers who worked for specific units, seen people cuffed, and I was taught to look straight and never look back at that person.

When I turned 16, in 2014. My parents gave me the news that we were moving to Carson. We moved a few months after that. Best thing? I got my own room and it's so quiet here, and the neighbors are friendly. But, want me to be honest? I actually miss the projects. Not because of all the things I've seen but because I knew what not to do. Plus, I got so used to the city and my friends, if I wanted to go to my friend's house, it was just a couple of buildings down. The mall was a few miles away. The store was down the street. The beach was a couple miles west. Life there was great because I found ways to enjoy my life.

The Culver City Projects.

It was all normal to me.

I Come From South Central

BY DANIEL GONZALEZ

I come from a block where I saw paramedics helping a guy who was stabbed in his back.

I come from a block that is in South Central.

I come from a block that is an hour away from school by car and two hours away on the Metro.

I come from a block where every time I get off the bus, coming from school, I'm afraid of being robbed while walking home.

I come from a block where the cops cruise by the front of my house.

I come from a block where I hear gunshots at 12:30 at night on 96th and Budlong. I live on 97th.

I come from a block where I hear arguing and screaming in the middle of the night.

I come from a block where a girl was killed on July fourth, just because she was wearing blue.

I come from a block where our house has an alarm so people won't break in.

I come from a block where my parents installed a metal gate, so people couldn't hop over it.

I come from a block where my dad was arrested in front of our own house because our alarm went off; the police thought he was the intruder.

I come from a block where I was accused of something I didn't do by my own "friends."

I come from a block where I don't trust anyone, not even my so called friends.

I come from a block in South Central where I'm afraid to stay.

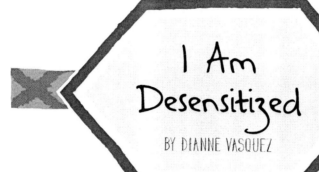

I Am Desensitized

BY DIANNE VASQUEZ

I am desensitized

I wonder how much poverty, violence and misery I can withstand

I hear gunshots, a kid crying out in pain because he's getting his butt whooped

I see dirty old palm trees, trash all around and half-dressed women waiting to turn a quick buck

I want to leave this 'hood,

but home is home

I am desensitized

I pretend that I don't grow nervous when too many cars slowly pass by

I feel unsafe past 8pm; can't even walk the block on my own

I worry that one day I will come back and everything will be gone

I am desensitized

I understand when people say try to make the best of any situation

But I say, "I live in South Central. What do you mean?"
I dream of moving away from danger, where I can be happy
I try to understand how things keep getting worse and worse
I hope to succeed in life but never forget where I'm from
I am desensitized

LONELY LATE NIGHT WALKS...
Photograph by Juanito Hernandez

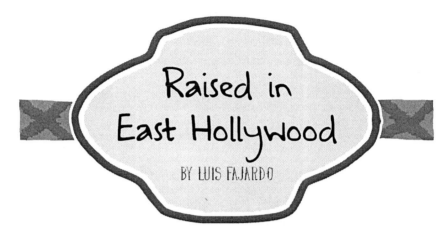

Raised in East Hollywood

BY LUIS FAJARDO

I was raised in East Hollywood in a low-income Hispanic neighborhood.

I was involved in the neighborhood gang and craved attention that I didn't receive from a loving mother or father.

So I raised myself and taught myself what I thought was right and what was wrong.

I taught myself that stealing was bad.

I taught myself that helping people in need of help is good, whether it's a blind person crossing the street or a senior citizen needing help with their marketing.

I lived in a world of violence and evil intentions.

For most of my life I lived without a father because he was too busy raising his other family.

My mom worked from dusk to dawn.

She was a manager at a Jack In The Box fast food restaurant in downtown L.A. She had no car but managed the nightshift without missing a day. She worked there for 12 years.

During the rare times she had a day off, she yelled at my sister for being rebellious and smoking cannabis.

As bad as my sister was, she was the only person I felt safe going to when I felt blue.

Probably explains why I'm rebellious and dependent on cannabis.

Whenever I felt alone and in my parents' absence I went to my sister and her smoking buddies. I turned to the euphoria of cannabis and alcohol when all I needed was a hug.

This was most of the time since my mom was too busy working and my dad was who knows where.

Every time my mom got mad and threw everything off the shelves, I turned to the euphoria of cannabis.

Every time I felt hurt, worried, stressed, scared or bored, I turned to cannabis.

Cannabis was easy to get hold of.
I was a kid, not yet a teenager, and I was blowing more smoke than the older cats in the neighborhood. Only to recap the previous high that had picked me up when I felt down.

I always felt better when I turned to cannabis.

I felt as if I had become my own therapist. Asking myself all these questions, like, "Why do I gang bang, why do I smoke, why are my grades F-U-U?" I would tell myself, "Next semester I won't smoke as much. Next semester I'll pass all my classes."

That never happened.

So I was convinced that getting high put me in a frame of mind that allowed me to cope with life, in and out of the 'hood.

Cannabis became my mother and father and taught me lessons along the way. Like who actually cares about you and not just your weed. The people who actually call you when you have no weed, those are the people who will dig you up out of the grave to ask, "How you doing, bro?"

Six years after I first lit up, I'm still using cannabis more than three times daily to relieve my stress.

I can't go a day without lighting up.

At least not without making a wrong decision out of frustration. My fuse is 9/10ths shorter when I'm not high.

Yes, to you I might be an addict, but I consider myself dependent on cannabis. Everyone is dependent on something, whether it's coffee, TV, music, your car…

I grew to love this plant like someone loves his mother.

Cannabis has shaped my life.

Cannabis helped me grow the courage to talk to the girl who is now my girlfriend, the girl I love.

Cannabis opened my mind and I was able to look farther than the problem or issue at hand. Rather than putting my head down and looking at all the negativity I was in, I looked past it, looked at what is to come. I looked for the smallest possible thing I can do to get me out of the gutter.

I now appreciate the small things in life. Thanks to cannabis.

LUIS FAJARDO
Portrait by Chris Wright

Where I Live

BY DANIEL GONZALEZ

I live on 97th Street and Budlong, where neighbors say, "Lots of history on Budlong. People get jumped, robbed, shot."

I live a few blocks from where a Blood was killed by a Crip and that's when "The 100 Days and Nights" began. Which meant the Bloods were going to kill people who weren't from our neighborhood for the next 100 days.

In my neighborhood or any part of South Central, we thank the Lord for another day.

My parents are putting our house up for sale because in the fall I'm off to Cal State Northridge, and we don't want to live here anymore.

I'm tired of living here!

I arrive late to school almost every day, then take a two-hour Metro ride home. And as I arrive home, I see and hear the problems and drama taking place in the streets.

Recently, several LAPD and detectives approached a neighbor's house at six a.m. and banged on their front door. They were asking if people had seen a suspect hanging around.

My neighborhood is diverse. Latinos, Blacks, Asians and even whites live here. But there are also drug dealers, alcoholics, thieves, and maybe even killers lurking about.

That's why in my neighborhood when friends and neighbors see each other we say, "Stay up." Which means, keep your head up and be aware of your surroundings all the time.

Because, sadly, we never know what might happen next.

Relentless

BY MAYNOR CALLETAN

I come from a place of darkness.
South Central is filled with violence, drugs and countless illegal activities
Where gangs recruit the young and cut their lives short.
From a momma who's devoted her life to her children.
Who attempts to shield them from the dangers of the community.
From a father whose ambitions cost him the joy of watching his kids grow up.
I come from the blue and white my brothers wear with pride
From the Friday night lights and the early morning practices
From victories and defeats.
I come from multiple families
One I was born into, and another I chose to join.
I come from those who don't give up no matter the challenge.
I come from those who are relentless.

I Am From The Projects

BY ELSA RAMIREZ

I am from the projects
I wonder when I will move the f— out of here
I see a place filled with guns, drugs and violence
I want to be different from everyone else around here because
where I come from no one seems to make it out
I am from the projects

I pretend to be carefree because where I'm from there's no
such thing as feelings
I feel ashamed of where I live
I worry that I'm never going to make it out of this place
I cry because there's no such thing as peace when you live in
the hood
I am from the projects

I understand that nobody can teach me how to make it out of
the ghetto
I say, "Some day I'll take my parents out of here."
I dream of becoming rich
I hope to be a successful person and be able to say, "I finally
made it out of the hood."
I am from the projects.

WHO WE ARE

HOW DO YOU SEE THE WORLD?
Photograph by Juanito Hernandez

She Knew Where She Was Going

BY GLORIOUS OWENS

She sees the world as a disgustingly beautiful place. Her life was planned the moment she turned three, December 30, 2000.

She was already aware, knew that her dad liked to cheat and her mom hated to work but had to bring home for her three girls.

This three-year-old girl saved up so much money. Her uncle would take $35 every month and deposit it in her bank account. She rose early every morning and woke the eight people she grew up with. She was an early riser and the first to go to bed. She was alert to everything around her.

She saw the tears streaming down her mother's face as she prayed to find a way to pay the rent.

She saw the anger on her mother's face when she had seen all the work her daughter hadn't completed. Her mom was confused. She was sure she had helped her daughter with that work.

She was tired of everyone looking down on her because she wasn't the first or even second born.

She was tired of always having to fight for her mom and dad's attention.

She set a goal of becoming better than everyone, no matter who doubted her.

She played basketball, would be the first woman in the NBA, would buy her whole family a house where they could all live.

She wanted to be a lawyer, make a good living, marry one day.

But dreams die hard.

She lives in South Central on 115th and Hoover.

She struggles to get a scholarship for volleyball.

Applications are stressing her out.

She's looking for a job to support herself because she will soon turn 18.

Don't get her wrong.

She knows sometimes hard work doesn't pay off, but being her stubborn, prideful self, she never imagines giving up. It's not in her DNA, not the way she was raised.

And it most definitely isn't her name.

Glorious Owens

Strong…that's who she is…

…Beautiful, fearless, and smart.

At least that's what her dad always told her.

GLORIOUS OWENS
Portrait by Chris Wright

Done

BY IONA SCOTT

I am drowning
in my own thoughts.
I am confused
in this world of ignorance.
I am lost
in my own home.
I am hurt
by those who say they care.
I am tired
of trying, only to get nowhere.
I am thrown off
by the words that lead one way,
yet mean another.
I am frustrated
with giving my all
to only get 10% back.
I am at ease
with things I shouldn't be okay with.
I am comfortable
with people who challenge me.
I am dying
to see who will stay.

And of those who say they'll stay,
who will go?
I am anxious
to be happy, genuinely.
I am hoping
things will only get better.
I am clinging
on to things that stay the same.
I am spiteful
for the things that change.
I am giving up
on the things that slowly drift away.
I am grabbing
on to the stuff that hurts me most.
I am trying
to grasp on to stuff that I shouldn't.
I am losing
my sanity oh-so slowly.
I am starting
to realize how unfair life is even to those who wait.

I am crying
over things that shouldn't cause so many tears.
I am clutching
to things that everyone else can let go of so easily.
I am ripping
away at my own brain
because the darkness only hurts me more.
I am pushing
because my whole life that's what I've been good at.

I am killing

myself over people

who wouldn't do the same for me.

I am holding

back from the things that should help me succeed.

I am wandering

through broken pieces

that I shouldn't have to put together in the first place.

I am over

everything.

I am so

done.

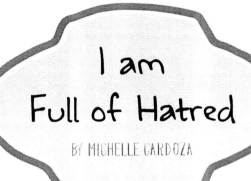

I am Full of Hatred

BY MICHELLE CARDOZA

I am full of hatred
I wonder if he hates himself
I hear his apologies day after day
I see his hands on my mother's neck
I want these memories to disappear
I am full of hatred

I pretend I love him
I feel his hand on my leg
I touch the dial pad, and think 9-1-1
I worry about seeing him again
I cry realizing my stepfather is a psycho
I am full of hatred

I understand everything happens for a reason
I say, "He's gone; he won't come back."
I dream of his killing us.
I try to forgive him; it's not happening.
I hope my father beats him good.
I am full of hatred.

Acceptance

BY COLBIE WITHERSPOON

If there is one thing that I hate most, it's people trashing me for my sexual orientation. When I was a little boy, I always knew that I would never love girls. I always knew myself in my skin, yet I always denied that I was gay. My friends who knew me always asked, "Colbie, when are you finally going to come out of the closet?" but I always said, "I love girls. Girls are cute."

Some days at school I was punked and bullied for being gay. I love who I am. Nobody can ever take that away from me.

In 7th and 8th grade my friends loved me and I told them I was bisexual, not gay. I was still denying the fact that I was gay. I watched the TV show *Degrassi High*. There were two gay football players, and watching the show, I started to realize a little more that it was okay to be who I was. One of the boys was open and didn't care what anyone thought of him. Another one denied he was gay and went to dances with girls but kissed boys.

Once I entered high school, it was a whole new ballgame. Kids called me "faggot" and "gay bop," and all the other names that made me feel like crap. In 9th grade I struggled and never wanted to come out. People were always starting rumors that I was gay, and those rumors started breaking me down. I needed help, fast.

The help I received was beneficial, and as I began 10th grade, people still did what they'd always done, but I ignored them and stuck up my middle finger and said, "Go to hell."

Eleventh grade was a self-defining year. I fell in love with a boy who was my "type." He was everything I wanted in a boy, but I made the mistake of calling him fake, and that ended our friendship. He told me he was done with me. I took it to heart. I harmed myself and contemplated suicide, and that led me to get serious about therapy.

All through 2015, I thought about him. He attended another high school but transferred to Venice this year.

Every time I see him I remember all that happened last year. I do miss him still, but I don't want anything to do with him.

In my senior year now, I have fully come into my own. I know who I am and nobody can change my mind. I am set on what I want for myself—a career in business management so that I can run a Boys & Girls Club.

I've Talked Everywhere*

BY DESIREE MILLER

A friend said to me, "Dez, you talk a lot."
And I said, "I know. Get used to it."
I've talked everywhere, bruh.
I've talked everywhere.
I've talked on stage. I've talked inside a tunnel and underneath the playground.
I've talked at pep rallies and I've talked where you shouldn't make a sound.
I've talked on TV and on radio.
I've talked at home and on the phone.
I've talked when my teacher said, "Don't."

I've talked everywhere, bruh.
I've talked everywhere.
I've talked in Arizona, View Park and Crenshaw.
I've talked in Arkansas, Texas, Florida and Washington.
I've talked on a floor where the carpet smelled like 'Smores.

I've talked on a plane. I've talked in my sleep.
I've talked under the bed where the monsters creep.
I've talked to a mime on the street—he didn't say much.

I've talked into a fan to make my voice sound funny.
I've talked to homeless people on the bus, some folks call them bummy.

I've talked everywhere, bruh.
I've talked everywhere.
I've talked at NBA and WNBA games.
I've talked so much it drove people insane.
I've talked at NFL stadiums and NHL rinks.
I've talked so much that I can finish a sentence before you blink.
I've talked at seminars and lectures while falling asleep.
I've talked in gang neighborhoods and in dark alleys.
I've talked in Venice while my mouth was full of Saby's.

I've talked everywhere, bruh.
I've talked everywhere.
I've talked on top of a Ferris wheel.
I've talked on a movie set.
I've talked while my friends placed some bets.
I've talked inside the East and West Gyms
I've talked when my mouth was filled with phlegm.
I've talked in a go-kart and on a motorcycle.
I've talked in a truck, on a scooter, skateboard, and bicycle.
I've talked while falling off all those vehicles.
I've talked way too much these past few years.
I've got a motor mouth.
But my voice is music to my ears.

I've talked everywhere, bruh.
I've talked everywhere.

*Based on the song *I've Been Everywhere* written by Geoffrey Mack in 1959, adapted by Hank Snow, made famous by Johnny Cash.

The "F" that Beat the Rest

BY BRIAN CAMPOS

After school on the ground, looking like a young bum was Brian.

Stupid kid looking for something to do.

Go figure, he checked out his history class.

There he found his crazy AP World History teacher, Ms. P, working furiously on papers, scratching them up with her little blue ink pen.

Brian walked to the back of the classroom, fell into a chair and looked at his week-late assignment.

Thirty minutes later he turned it in.

Surprise, surprise.

Ms. P graded it in minutes, called him over, said, "Brian, you're going to fail this class, but I want you to try again next year. You're lazy, but you understand the basics here enough to do really well on the AP World History exam."

So every Wednesday for the next six months, Brian headed over to Ms. P's classroom after school. And studied.

By year's end his "shooting star" classmates hated him.

And for good reason.

Brian kicked their 3-out-of-5 butts with a 4 on the AP World History Exam.

And he infuriated the one girl who scored a 5 because a guy "so dumb" almost beat her untouchable score.

And yet, he still earned an "F" in AP World History.

Who Am I?

BY BIANCA LOPEZ

My name is Bianca and I'm the girl known as B.

Seven years ago my whole life changed, and not in a good way but in a horrible way. It felt like someone stabbed their hands inside me and took my soul.

Seven years ago is when I told myself that this world had nothing for me anymore, that my life was done; but something told me that I had to keep my head up and live through it, that everything was going to be okay. All I had to do was smile and be happy. That was the only way I fooled people into believing that nothing was wrong with me.

January 29th, 2011 was the day God took my auntie away from all her suffering and a week later my brother was thrown in prison.

What had I done to deserve something like that? It was a tough time for me. I didn't eat, didn't want to talk to anyone, I didn't go to school for almost a month, and when I did I was distant from everyone. I was embarrassed and feeling so many emotions.

After a few months, I realized that I was glad that God took my auntie because she's in a better place and she's not suffering anymore, but one thing that I wasn't glad about was my brother. He had the choice to do something right and he backed away from the whole situation! The only job he had was to be a brother and to be the greatest role model and he failed at that! I was angry at my brother for a while because I needed a brother to help me with homework and be there for me! All I had was a brother in prison who is now hoping he can get out soon.

Seven years ago I was this one shy, scared, hidden girl stuck in a box crying out for help.

Seven years ago people knew me as this girl who was always smiling and happy, but they didn't know the person behind that happiness and smile.

I never spoke about where I am from or the struggles I had because I didn't want anyone to feel pity for me or judge me.

Acceptance

BY ZENAIDA JIMENEZ

All my life I felt left out because of my skin color.

I was always the darkest skinned among my friends. At 11, I felt uncomfortable around my classmates because I was the darkest student in the room. I would only feel better, slightly better, when a new student who was darker than me entered our class.

One year I counted all the darker skinned students in my class. Four. Yet, I still felt that I did not belong or fit in with the rest of the school.

In addition to my dark skin, I had hairy arms and in middle school developed acne. I despised looking down at my arms, my legs. Sometimes I would look in the mirror and burst out crying.

My mother never had a clue that I held such self-hating thoughts. And as a kid I often thought I had a pile of dirt on my skin so whenever I showered, I would scrub so hard I left red marks all over my body.

In third grade my entire class was walking back from some activity when two girls approached a kid named Diego and said something that offended him. I couldn't imagine what they had said that so upset him. So I asked him, and he said that the girls wanted to know why I was so dark and hairy.

I felt speechless, ashamed.

Part of me wanted to slap them; part of me wanted to cry. But I did neither. What I did was develop more self-hatred for that which was naturally part of me: my flesh.

It took years but I managed to see the beauty of my skin tone. I came to realize it didn't matter how dark or light I was. What mattered was that I had learned to accept myself and see the beauty in myself. Now, I love my skin tone.

It doesn't bother me anymore, or maybe I should say, as much, that I'm one of the darkest students in my class as well as among my friends.

When I look back at pictures of my younger self I realize that I left the demons and negativity inside my head to think the worst of myself.

Now I see the positivity of my color.

Now, when I see something of myself in the mirror that I once hated I think that it's only the image, the reflection of what the devil inside wanted me to see.

I am Emotionally Destroyed

BY KEI-ARRI McGRUDER

I am emotionally destroyed
I wonder how my future will turn out
I hear screams, cries, laughs
I see blood, tears, love
I want answers
I am emotionally destroyed

I pretend that I'm ok and happy, but
I feel like I'm fading away
I touch my face, wondering what others see
I worry that I am not enough
I cry knowing he never wanted to be there
I am emotionally destroyed

I understand life is f—ed up
I say, "I'll get out of this (I am never having kids)"
I dream nothing. My dreams are black, then I wake up
I try to make it through my ghetto day
I hope I will be free of my personal chains one day
I am emotionally destroyed

KEI-ARRI MCGRUDER
Portrait by Doris Longman

Pretty Bird

BY KATHERINE SEGAIDA

She expanded her wings to her nearest best
Because she felt as if she was nothing but less
She flew away from the dark shade before the lights fade to a
darker shade
Tree is so high so she wondered how she'd fly
She'd fall but she'll fly right back up with her broken wing
Until one day she fell, couldn't fly
Wings so broken all she did was cry
Until another birdie came with new set of wings
So she could forget about her old dark wings
With those new set of wings all she has ever been
Was a pretty bird with a dark set of thin strings
That won't weigh her down and every now
And then, all you'll see is pretty bird with her new set of wings.

Inspire To Be Inspired

BY JOHN BEMBRY

Only Got a Dollar in my pocket,
Running these streets not an option.
Get caught up like these women, wonder who is the father.
Wonder who is the Author?
Steelo. The face and the voice of the ghetto.
Inglewood to be Exact.
Back pack raps now.
Working with these perfect verses.
Get hit with the hook.
Kimbo Slice with the delivery, I'm more than nice.
Mr. Mic with the God Flow.
Paint pictures like a Picasso,
Or Jay-Z, Whoever!
My Hieroglyphs survive through any weather.
Read between the words.
My tongue carries the power.
Get devoured by the verse.
Ugh. Police, Number one hated, debated, and doubted.
People around me
Wasn't impressed until I said F the World.

Now they saying I'm next.
I don't need a Hand out.
I do it for the Craft.

I do it for the pain and the sorrow.
Today and tomorrow.
Never let them see you sweat.
Until your day is up, in this game of lust.
I do it for the pain and the sorrow.
Today and tomorrow.
Never let them see you sweat.
Until your day is up, in this game of lust.

Inspire to be Inspired.
Inspire to be Inspired.
Inspire to be Inspired.
Inspire to be Inspired.

I been on my way for a long time now.
Graduated high school made my mom proud.
Still rolling the dice, life a gamble.
Will I be successful or will I see shackles?
A cell, walking earth but we living hell.
To fail is misery upon everyone you tell.
A hill we coming toward,
think back to move forward,
be scared and face horror,
be high and feel sober.
I'm closer to my death than to my dreams.
I'm feeling a little old,
Right now I'm twenty.

Did a lot of things for my age,
there's things I haven't seen.
Skin all Tatted Bubbasteeze love Ink. Man!
Chuck Taylors, I'm eating my Now and Laters,
Inspire to be inspired.
I'm doing people a favor.
All the motivation,
I get it from self creation.
One of these days I really got to make it.
I tell them.
Inspire to be Inspired.
Thank to be alive.
Fight against the odds.

Crown with no power
Yeah.
Young people, learn to grow equal,
Real I know listen.
Why would I lie?
Inspire to be Inspired.
Thank to be alive.
Fight against the odds.
Crown with no power
Yeah.
Young people, learn to grow equal,
Real I know listen.
Why would I lie?

Inspire to Be inspired.
Inspire to be Inspired.

JOHN BEMBRY

Portrait by Chris Wright

NOT THE ONLY ONE

My Life
BY KATHERINE SECAIDA

Kat's two worlds are alike, both filled with pain. POPS and family are different.

I feel like my family doesn't understand where I am coming from, but they know one thing: I am hurting. But they tell me I shouldn't be crying about anything because I have a mother who isn't an addict. No matter how stressful her life, her answer is always, "drugs are not the answer."

On the other hand, POPS is the place where it is fine to cry and listen to people's advice and not feel crazy and where it's okay to talk about the past and what still haunts you.

These two worlds may crash into each other, but I'm scared of the damage it will cause if they do. Am I ready to see my mother cry? No, I don't want her to. My dad has hardly been in my life for over 15 years. My older sister, Maria, was into the drug/popping pills phase when she was my age. I feel like all my life there's been some type of drug memory. Maria was hurt and looked for drugs but grew away from it and has her life together. I look up to her. And then there's me who is always aggressive, hurt, and who saw drugs as an escape but that hurt my mind.

My POPS world helps me get through my past. At first it was hard to write about my life, but I learned not to feel ashamed of my past and to just embrace it. POPS is my second home. The vibe is always open, and it's okay to cry and show emotion because we always have a shoulder to cry on. I don't think I would have had the courage to write if it wasn't for attending POPS and listening to peoples' stories. I relate to a lot of the teens who attend.

My family is my other world, but it's hard to talk about certain things with my mother. I can't talk to my sister at times because she's either at work or with her friends. My life can change, and it is changing, but there's always something in the way. That's when I get mad. My father was never there for 15 years—I went from visiting him in jail to visiting him in the hospital, and that had a big impact on my life. Now that I think about it, I sometimes feel "what the hell? What's next on your list?"

My two worlds will crash into each other someday, and I hope my family does not turn their backs on me because I do need help, and I am getting it. I don't want to see anyone being hurt anymore because I am a new person with changes and a new mindset.

POPS Memoir

BY MARIANA HERNANDEZ

Pain of the prison system, a life-changing moment of my sophomore year. Let's start from the beginning—how I even came to know about the club itself.

Beginning of sophomore year of high school, I was enrolled in Mr. Danziger's English class. Danziger happened to be one of my favorite teachers. He didn't force us to learn boring things. He made our class fun, letting us write daily about our day and ourselves. He feels it's important to write daily, personally, for ourselves. We all go through struggles and have to find some way out of those. My way out was writing.

One day towards the beginning of class, Danziger mentioned a club that he's in charge of along with his wife. It's called POPS and it takes place every Wednesday in Danziger's room. He told us POPS stands for Pain of the Prison System. It's a club that anyone with a family or friends who have been or are incarcerated is welcome to join. I started going to POPS with one of my best friends, Katherine. I wanted to support her. At first she wanted to go because her dad has been incarcerated multiple times and she needed to find a place for people to help her cope with the problems that affected her deeply. Katherine needed a place of caring and supportive adults and students.

We all have dark pasts—not just my best friend but everyone. Those pasts are like a dark, black cove full of secrets, an unknown and mystery to most people. Secrets are locked away and never shared. I had those secrets I never shared with anyone but myself, and on paper. I try to make sure I write it all down to release tension and stress.

When the time came to actually attend POPS, Kat asked me to go with her as a supportive best friend. Of course I came along. That Wednesday at lunch when I walked into the room, I wondered how these teens in high school would open up about problems they couldn't even tell their best friends about. But it was nothing for them. They had a courage I didn't understand. And that day my mindset changed. It was deeper than just opening up about our stories. Pretty soon I was attending the club not only to support Katherine but to support all those people sitting in the room with the guts to open up about their scariest, deepest, real stories. I had mad respect for them all.

I feel emotional and happy about what the club is offering people. Including myself. A friend. A place that feels like home. We have the most comfortable place to be open with everyone without being judged. Whether we are telling stories about drugs or being arrested for a crime, in that room we're able to tell them. These are the kinds of stories that are most difficult to tell, but the people of POPS tell their stories, and to me their opening up about their pain is so strong. I look up to these boys and girls who have stories to tell. I have a place that feels like home. POPS with Mr. Danziger and his wife,

Amy, probably changed my life. They taught me to feel okay about my dark past. I feel comfortable talking about it now and I'm happy to know I have positive people in my life—the students in POPS who I keep close to my heart.

I have a story in the 2015 POPS Anthology, and I'm proud to be in there along with the other amazing authors of *Ghetto By the Sea*. We're only high school authors, but the book leaves an impact on all our lives. There's a lot still to come. And I find it crazy how I got here—when Mr. Danziger first told me I could write about anything, positive or negative, it took me a while to think I could do that. I wondered if I could get really personal. Was I ready for people to read a little piece of my life? But then I realized if these other young people could do it, then I could too. And now that feeling of knowing my story is out there for everyone, including strangers, feels good. People I don't know will know what goes through my mind and how I feel about my past and the near future. When I heard anyone in the world could read our book, I felt content.

Everyone needs to know the importance of what we went through in life as children and teenagers. We have some perks and some not-so-good luck in our lives. But now I pick up my pen and grab my notebook and write away all my thoughts— happy, to deep and dark. It's just me and my writing, and this genuinely keeps me happy, even if I'm not the best writer. I do this for me, and I know it helps me through everything.

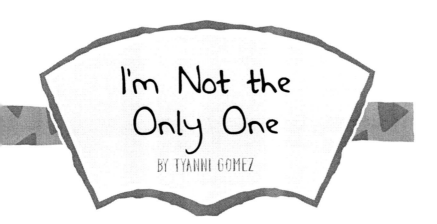

I'm Not the Only One

BY TYANNI GOMEZ

Everyone has a story.

POPS (Pain of the Prison System) is my story.

For a long time I felt trapped and didn't know how to escape my thoughts, many of which frighten me: the memories of my parents arguing with each other; my grandmother passing away; when I was bullied; suffering from depression; a heartbreak; my dad and I arguing over stupid stuff; my learning disabilities and bad choices I made.

I would sneak out, talk back, shut people out.

I punished myself with never ending "what if's," "remember when," and "I regret that."

I felt as though I couldn't tell anyone about anything. Plus, I assumed no one would understand or care. Or worse, they would think I was weak or just trying to gain attention.

Then, one Wednesday during my sophomore year at Venice High School I wandered into a POPS meeting. At lunch. In room 120.

On the board someone had written "First we eat."

That intrigued me.

And two steps further into the room I saw a feast of salads, pasta, chocolate croissants, and platters of pineapple, grapes, and cantaloupe.

I ate.

And ate.

Oh yeah. And there were exotic dark breads and baguettes from *Le Pain Quotidien* and bagels and M&M encrusted cookies from Panera Bread.

The assembled students talked about their lives, like what a family would or should do.

The club, POPS, is a support group for students whose lives have been impacted by incarceration, and it's run at Venice by Amy and Danziger. They're a married couple. Danziger's my English teacher. Amy is a professional writer. I had met her once before. When he introduced me, he told her I was a terrific writer.

At the meeting Danziger passed out paper and pens and told us to write. About anything.

I wrote and I wrote about things that had been bottled up inside me for years. All these feelings that I had stuffed deep inside exploded onto the page.

That was the moment I realized that writing was my passion.

I wrote about hurt; the people who had hurt me; how I'd hurt myself.

I felt as if that one writing session, that one paper is what cured me. Or began to heal me.

The other POPS students wrote too. Real feelings, truthful things spilled out onto their pages. Here it was okay to write what you felt. No one said "just get over it"

At these lunch meetings I feel safe, my thoughts are safe. I can write about anything. Free of judgement.

Outside the room I felt no one really cared because I was just a teenager.

But this was new. A place where I could come and feel multiple emotions cascading over one another in the same moment. Here, I felt happy, relieved, safe, loved.

And anyone who wanted could read their work aloud.

It was amazing that people like Kat, Veronica, Anthony, and Bianca stood at the podium and read essays about fathers who were in and out of prisons; fathers who refused to give up the gang life; teenagers being busted for selling weed; a family driving 24 straight hours to visit a son/brother in prison.

I learned that some of those who smile the brightest hurt the most.

I instantly respected them for that.

Danziger said, "Everyone has a story. Or a lot of stories."

My POPS family and I wrote our stories and poems, then emailed them to Amy who cleaned up our grammar, and they were anthologized in *Ghetto by the Sea*.

When I held that book in my hand I realized that we all have stories and we are never truly alone. And that our innermost thoughts need to be released onto the page. And into the world.

I am part of that book.

And that's how POPS saved me.

My best friend, Alyssa, once said, "You were there, but not really there."

She was right. I was not myself for a large chunk of my life.

And my other best friend, John, used to tell me, "Don't let the negativity get in your way." I listened to his words but never knew what actions to take to deal with my problems.

Until I walked into POPS.

Every Wednesday at 1:29 p.m. in Room 120, I am myself again.

The me I'm supposed to be.

My true self.

The one I love.

I Put My Life Together

BY KATHERINE SECAIDA

I am a new person, I may not be the smartest, but I know what's right for me. I know my value.

I know the feeling of being alone, I know how it feels to have your heart broken, I know how it feels to lose a parent mentally, I know the feeling of always watching your back from every angle, I know the feeling of being hand cuffed—being shoved into a cop car and being treated like a criminal, I know the feeling when you feel the rush in your fists and face but step back because you know what you are capable of doing, I know the feeling of carrying drugs in your backpack hoping you won't get caught, I know the feeling of having your own mother cry, and you're the reason why, I know the feeling of punching the wall, I know the feeling of crying at night and picking yourself up the next day and pretending nothing ever happened, I know that feeling of hopping over the fence fearing either you will get your jeans caught or be chased down. I know the feeling of hitting rock bottom.

I know the feeling of living that double life.

Growing up with gangs, fights, drugs, gunshots, living in the projects, it's always risk taking.

Growing up with oh, she's like my little sister or nah, I'm trying to hit that. You step out that door and step into the streets you never know if you'll make it home that night.

Don't go outside on those streets, Kathy!

Where are you going?

Who is that?

What's in your backpack?

What time are you getting home?

You better get your ass home, I'm not playing with you.

Words my mom would always repeat. She doesn't have to do that anymore

Mom, I'm sorry but you don't know what I've done in those two dark ages, 13 and 14, fights and drugs. I used to come home high and I used to hide everything from you until the day I got caught.

This is the LAPD, your daughter Katherine Secaida is at the Pacific Station for assault.

That is the day my life changed, age 13. It was time to wake the f___ up. Age 14, Mom, I tried to get myself together and you knew that because I cried and cried when you asked me what was wrong. I couldn't tell you everything. You only knew how my dad's addiction hurt me. Knowing I could be locked up scared me. Knowing my temper was dangerous scared me.

Age 15 to this day I will never forget the look in my mom's eyes when the words came out, "Katherine Secaida, case dropped, you're free to go." No juvenile hall time. No more bullshit.

Locked up or dead, those words shocked my mother but mostly they shocked me. I don't want to be locked up or dead.

I've stayed in school, I've been hanging out with positive friends and mostly my best friend Mariana. I know I have a shoulder to cry on. My second mother, Dana, who has watched over me ever since I was six, and just watching her kids grow made me feel like their big sister, and as they get older I will be their role model and help them out the way their mother helped me out. My 10th grader teacher, Mr. Danziger, who would always ask all these questions to make my story feel real.

POPS is my second home where I write and listen to other people's stories. It is life changing.

I put my life together. It's never too late.

AT EVERY DARK MOMENT IN MY LIFE
Photograph by Katherine Secaida

WE THE BRAVE

I Come from Fear

BY JAMEKA REYNOLDS

I come from fear.

I come from 3 a.m. calls to the cops because my mom is laid out in a puddle of blood.

I come from looking into her black eyes as she tells me that she still loves him.

I come from feeling afraid because my heart always gets walked on; I don't understand why.

I come from looking for acceptance in a man, my mom's ex-boyfriend, because my father was never there to give me the love I needed.

I come from growing up fast because being immature and a child gets you nowhere.

I come from the fear of losing my mom to her boyfriend and trying to break away knowing I'd have nothing and no one. I'd be alone, and on my own, leaving everything behind.

I come from short fatherless days, and long motherless nights.

I come from not letting anyone close to me because I fear company.

I come from the place where music silences my thoughts, words become absent from my mouth, and my smile hides my pain.

I come from the fear of not knowing if I'll wake up one day and everything I've worked hard for will be gone.

I come from trying to live in my future because the present keeps leading me to the past.

I come from where being strong becomes a mood and smiling is only a cover up.

I come from a little place called fear, and it's hard to explain what is here, but I'm here.

I come from fear.

She Did Have a History

BY KHYRA BLACK

She did have a history.

Her father was an alcoholic. And her mother worked from 8 in the morning till 7 at night to provide a roof over her head and food on the table.

She writes words on a paper in hopes that she will one day understand. Maybe one day she will understand why her dad is an alcoholic. She watched him walk around with pants drenched in pee and head hung low and eyes barely open because the hangover was too unbearable. But she always hugged him when he said "Sorry." She forgave him, every time. And it's crazy, because he almost killed her once.

Driving her in the car on the freeway, high on pills and drunk on liquor. Swerving left and right, her head hitting the window, laughing because at first it was funny. At first it was a joke. She didn't know. She had no clue. She had no clue that he was drunk. She had no clue that he would fall asleep sitting in the driver's seat, pulled over on the side of Interstate 15.

She had no clue he would say "Sorry" again. And that she would forgive him. She forgives a lot, but she never forgets. She has cried a lot. She has fought for her grades. She has fought for her happiness. She has fought for her. She prays for everything she has. Her praying makes her stronger. And God makes her wiser.

"Lord, please give me strength to overcome obstacles in my life. Whether it is of You, to make me stronger or of the evil one who tries to knock me down. Despite it all, Satan's evil works will not prevail, for the battle is already won and I shall overcome. In Jesus' name, I pray."

Amen.

I'm Only a Child

BY MADISON ABERCROMBIE

"Your mother has cancer."

My mother delivered this line to my sisters and me in third person. I can't remember the exact day she spoke those words, but I remember my exact feelings.

My eyes welled up, but being afraid to hurt my mother's feelings I tried my hardest not to cry.

When she spoke those words, dozens of thoughts and questions invaded my mind, but just as quickly my mind went blank.

I stared at Danielle, my younger sister, age four, who held my six-year-old sister Jasmine's hand. Danielle's other hand was balled into a fist. Jasmine had been dealing with bullies at school. Now she had this. And we all had to deal with a dad who was in and out of prison.

"How bad is it?" Jasmine asked.

"Is your hair going to fall out?" Danielle asked. And then, "Mommy, are you going to die?"

By ages 5, 6 and 7 we sisters knew how to bus from San Pedro to downtown Los Angeles where we went to an ATM machine and withdrew hundreds of dollars at a time.

We knew how to take the food stamps card across the street to buy the whole family's weekly groceries.

Though still in elementary school, we were considered adults.

But we were only children trying to deal with our reality, being poor, white and living in a ghetto neighborhood.

What once were daily activities, like playing tag with Mommy, quickly became memories of a distant past. And Daddy's absences, he could be gone for days or even months, became normal.

"He did meth!" my mother screamed at me.

2008. My dad was locked up for doing meth and picking up a prostitute.

I was close to my dad and it became difficult for me to accept the fact that we would never be as close as we once were.

He wrote all of us saying how sorry he has.

I wrote back in secret, but my mom always burned my letters and said they didn't get through or they were lost in the mail.

I lost hope of ever playing football with my dad or telling knock-knock jokes.

Defending my dad's actions and fighting with my mom over them also became the norm.

In 2008, when I was eight years old, Jasmine suddenly shut Danielle and me out of her life. She tried blocking out all the pain and discovered it was easier not to care, which gave me the additional responsibility of coping with my little sister's feelings.

"I have surgery again today."

It's 2010. And my mom is both a cancer patient and a student at UCLA.

My sisters and I were thrilled that she was accepted into college, but also worried because one day she collapsed walking up the steps to class.

It was also in 2010 that my mother went through chemo again.

"The first time didn't work! Why will it work the second time?" I demanded.

I was terrified of losing her.

Earlier she had been through radiation and had an ovary removed.

The doctors were taking her apart piece by piece. And I was afraid my outgoing, single mom would die from all the surgeries, and her jobs and her school work. She was trying too hard to build a life for her daughters.

"I wish I could die!"

2012 and Danielle began suffering from depression. She was so sad from the life she leads.

"I'm so sorry, girls" my mother said, as if the cancer were somehow her fault.

"I can't do this anymore!" I screamed at my sisters. I wanted to die. I hate this life.

"Why us?" I asked.

I feared I would lose my mother to cancer and my kid sister to darkness.

"If this doesn't work, I can't go on anymore," my mother said to me one day when I met her on her lunch break.

2014. I am 14 and I realized I would never be happy as long as my mother suffered from cancer.

I also realized that without my sisters I wouldn't be here today.

I figured that my problem was not my mother's illness, but the way I chose to deal with it.

My dad was in and out of prison, and Jasmine pretended I didn't exist and Danielle lived in sadness. And then I had to take on the responsibility for my stepbrothers. I was over-whelmed and looked for a way out.

"Why are you doing this?" my mother and my stepdad screamed at me.

I was high.

I didn't care what they said.

At 15 I started drinking and smoking to numb the pain.

I rebelled against the cancer cells growing inside my mother's body as if they could respond to my rebellious actions.

But later in my fifteenth year I stopped the self-destructive behavior.

Today I realize that my life isn't easy, but it's not impossible.

I can cope with my mother's illness. And a dad who is in and out of my life.

And yes, it's a lot to deal with.

A whole lot for a fifteen-year-old.

I understand it could be worse, but it could also be a lot better.

Maybe one day, slowly, things will improve.

And deep down, I think they will.

Juanito Hernandez
Portrait by Chris Wright

The Girl You Think You Know

BY YESENIA GOMEZ

The girl you think you know isn't the girl you know. The girl you see every day laughing and smiling isn't really happy. The girl you think has a perfect life cries herself to sleep. The girl you see wears long sleeves to hide her scars. The girl you see brave and strong is actually dying on the inside. The girl you see every day has fought more battles than you can imagine. That girl thinks that she is weak. That girl thinks that she is worthless. The girl you see walking down the hall with her friends telling a funny story, she is telling the story of her uncle arrested for sexual abuse against her. She comes across as annoying but she is more mature than you will ever know. That girl had to grow up by the age of four because her mom was in jail, and she lived with her aunt, dad and grandma. She had to grow up because by six she was a foster child and had to look out for herself. She had to do all this alone because she had no siblings and her foster parents treated her like she was one of those children who ask for money in the streets.

That girl you see with the light brown eyes has cried more tears than you can imagine. You say you know what true pain is, but you don't. True pain is when you smile just to

stop the tears from falling. True pain is when you have to go away because your parents screwed up. True pain is when you have to live with families that aren't yours and watch them laughing and making memories and moments that will last a lifetime. But the most painful thing in the whole world is when you think you'll return to your old life when in reality after you have gone through all this stuff, nothing will ever be the same.

Theme from English B*

BY MADISON ABERCROMBIE

The instructor said,
  Go home tonight and write
A page tonight
And let that page
Come out of you....
Then it will be true.

I understand the way it should be...
And I understand the way it's not.

Four white walls, two doors, my closet and my bedroom door.
A TV that's turned on ten hours a day. Or more.
A window that is as tall as I am,
And as wide as two people lying side by side.

I stare at the streetlights just outside my window,
The only light that brightens my room.
I hear three hard knocks against my bedroom door,
But I don't crawl down the ladder of my bunk bed.
Two more knocks,
And this time they grow louder

I sit and stare, blink once
And then simply close my eyes.

I feel my eyes puff up as I try harder to control my breathing.
I think about my life.
I focus on the good.

As I try harder and harder to think of the good,
It becomes harder and harder to breathe.

I open my eyes but my crying continues.
I cradle my knees in my arms and fall to the right,

I grab the closet handle.
I grab a life-sized stuffed bear and move it closer to me.

I lay my head on its bowling ball-sized head.

I throw my left leg over the bear's stomach,
I cry some more.
I can no longer breathe; I pant.

My lungs hurt as my breath leaves my body.
My eyes sting as tears drip down my face.
It all feels as if there is no peace;
That my world is falling apart
This is the feeling of me feeling helpless.

I hear my bedroom door opening.
My sister rushes to my bed and hurries up the ladder
She sits beside me.
She raises her arms.
She pets my head,

Then moves closer.

I feel her fear.
I feel her heart pounding faster and faster,
She fears holding me,
Fears I will push her away.

I hear her steady breathing becoming less steady
She grabs my shoulder,
Then my head,
She gently places my head on her chest.

I hear her heartbeat accelerating,
Then slowing as I hold her tightly.

I feel her relief as I allow her to comfort me.

She brushes my hair behind my ears and kisses the top of my
head.

"It'll be okay, I'm here. It has to get worse before it gets better.
This is just our lives, now. Okay? This is just what we came
from. This isn't us; this isn't what we are. I promise."

She whispers this to me as she holds my hand,
Kisses my forehead.

She grabs my pillow and adjusts it to the back of her head.
She holds my hand and strokes my head as I close my eyes.

I come from a place where my sisters are my mentors.

I come from a dad who didn't have bad luck or bad timing.

I come from a dad who did drugs and left us behind to become

A bum, cigarette smoking, meth loving "Son of God,"
As he tells my sisters and me,
Expecting us to forgive everything he's done.

I come from a career mom.
A woman who returned to college at age 34
To create a better world for her children.

I come from UCLA Family Housing.

I come from, "It can only get better."
As all my close friends say,
But feeling heartbroken
When it gets worse.

*Based on a poem by Langston Hughes

Power to the People

BY KEI-ARRI MCGRUDER

I have the power to rise up
Power to me, power to you
My brothers and sisters we must rise up, for what we need for what we believe
What happened to the dream of Dr. King?
That dream was not only for people who looked like me, but for people of all different complexions
Power to you, power to me
Stop all this getting pregnant at 16 and buried before you even hit 18
Make them see that we are much more than a statistic talking about 1-out-of-3
Please, tell me, what I'll turn out to be just because of assumptions and test scores that you believe relate to my ethnicity
Power to you, power to me
We are much greater than what we've made out of this 21st century
Power to you, power to me
I'm only 17 but I seen some skittish things that I wish I could change dearly but all I did was stand silently

Please stop this gang-banging thing, it's unnecessary to fight over some color you wanna be or a location that has no real connection with your own history

And the people you chill with won't even have the slightest sympathy when you get shot down cold

But maybe some beer will be poured out on the ground talking about rest in peace to the dead bros

Then they go on living it up every day while you 6 feet under in a grave

Power to you, power to me

My brothers and sisters, we need to stay focused on our dream and not on these foolish things like trying to be somebody's trap queen or selling weed

Use your brain wisely

Because, my beautiful queens, that body won't take you very far, trust me; and my handsome kings, sports are not the only things that can help you get out of the low embolden society

We need to educate the 21st century and make a better future for our children to be

Power to you, power to me

Power to you, power to me

Power to you, power to me

We will rise up and finish his dream just wait and see!

My Faith To Freedom

BY LESLIE MATEOS

It's a hard life, I hear promises of freedom,
I look up and down to the left and to the right,
But freedom is nowhere to be found.
It was all just a dream,
A dream that lit up my night.
But there is still hope inside of me.
Hope that will never disappear.
Hope that tells me there will be a time
when my freedom will come
And I'll be free,
Free of all the pain.

LOOKING FORWARD, LOOKING BACK

I REFLECT ON MY LIFE TOO MUCH
Photograph by Juanito Hernandez

Transition

BY VALERIA DE LA TORRE

As I transition into a young adult, I look back at what I have learned.

I'm not the only one with a f__ed up world.

I'm not the only one holding back words that are worth being heard.

I'm more than just a brown girl, I won't live the way they want me to,

Oppressed and without a word.

I have learned that this world is twisted but I could make some difference.

Breaking stereotypes and doing things differently.

I know we're raised with little and given limits but I won't let that faze me.

I will succeed because of the two people who have raised me with hopes of giving them the world, even if they want nothing in return.

I won't be brought down by the hate around me

I will only rise with the love surrounding me.

KATHERINE SECAIDA AND JAYVON MURRAY
Portrait by Chris Wright

I Come From

BY JESSICA DE LA MORA

I come from a family of four.
Where my father has been in prison since the year 2003
a sister that is 21-years-old but doesn't care about anyone but
herself and her boyfriend.
A mother that divorced her husband while he was in prison
when my father was already dealing with the pain and hurting of his mother dying.

I come from living in a nice beautiful house, but that is lonely
and quiet inside.
I come from not wanting to be home because of the feeling of
not being wanted there.
I come from a stepfather living there but that's always grumpy
and in his room.
Where my mother gets home, showers, and goes to bed.
I come from having a 30-minute conversation with my mother
in the morning, going to school, then another 30 minutes
after coming from my aunt's house to home in the night time.

Those are the only times I have a conversation with my
mother, to catch up.

I come from my mother asking me, "How's school?"
Lying and saying I'm doing great just to make her proud.
I come from my mom telling me I can always go to her to talk
Yet I'm scared for her to judge me or get mad about decisions I made.

I come from a tattooed father that is now in prison
I come from getting my hopes up on him being out here for my high school graduation
Having my dad and mother cheering my name and having tears of joy.

I come from wanting more in life
wanting to go to Stanford University
I come from smoking weed during the week and partying with alcohol on the weekends
I come from wanting to stay out of my own home to avoid the sadness
wanting to get a car by this summer to leave the house any time I want
I come from waiting to turn 20 years old to move out of my mother's house
I come from a handful of regrets, decisions, and mistakes.

But in reality, what I say out loud
"I come from a great, perfect family and wouldn't trade my life for anyone else's"
Now that is one of the biggest lies I have told
I am Jessica De La Mora.

Learning from Your Mistakes

BY TANIA CRUZ

He grew up loved by his mom but never by his dad. There was always sadness in his eyes. Growing up was hard, yet he tried to keep his head up for his mom's sake. Things got tough, and the only choice he saw was joining a gang to make money and ease his pain. But that never works out, and he was caught with a gun. Ended up in prison, leaving two children behind. He has years before he gets out. His mom cries every night hoping to have her child back in her arms. There's nothing his mom can do but sit and cry. Now he sits behind the walls trying once again to keep his head up. No one really knows what's going on with him behind the walls. He learned from his mistakes, but he knows the wisdom came too late.

Is This What My Parents Warned Me About?

BY D. JONES

I'm 18 now. Less than a month left before I graduate high school. Time to get to know the "real world."

Honestly, I'm afraid of what's next. I know what to expect, I think. But I'm not so sure if it'll pan out as planned. I was supposed to be a statistic a long time ago. I'm 18, that's a milestone in life growing up where I come from. I broke the cycle. No, I'm not a gang member. Sadly, all of my friends except a few of us got jumped in and are in jail. Thank God I have yet to lose any of them, permanently. No one is dead. But I can't be too worried about them. I have to become a man now. Find a job. Buy a house and car. Have a family. And everything else that's so broadly advertised yet hard to maintain.

I have an idea of what I want to do in life. Play professional ball? Sure. Highly unlikely, closest thing to impossible, but I'll play as long as I can. Realistically speaking. Not sure what I want to major and minor in just yet. Metaphysics? Business? Real Estate? Sports Therapy? I don't know. I'm a minority. The U.S. is set against my kind. I'm not supposed to make it. Some say I have the power to finish my one man's dream, Martin

Luther King Jr.'s, that is. Big shoes to fill. I think about wanting to lead my people towards something greater. But how can I lead something that breaks itself? In no way are Blacks united. We kill each other all day over a color on a block. For us to prevail as a race, we must become one. Unite. Everybody wants to be better than the next, and here we are.

I've thought about dropping out. I've thought about selling drugs. I'll get nowhere without my education, although I feel that they teach us bullshit 95% of the time. I've been misled. School is meant to turn us into robots and work 9-to-5's for someone else. And I'll never want to purposefully hurt anyone, so I won't sling a rock. I've seen what kind of fast money that'll make. Also seen how quickly your life it'll take. I feel I'm stuck in a bind. Sometimes I even question existence. It could be some dream or just a feeble imagination.

Yeah, I want to get rich. Who doesn't? Money is nonexistent, the government runs it. Slavery was abolished in 1865, so they say. I'd like to live as lavishly as possible and enjoy life. I would also LOVE to give back to my community, charity, to help worldwide. Put my money somewhere it'd make a change. If Queen Elizabeth can cure world hunger four times and still be rich, why doesn't she?

As long as I have my family and good health, I'm richer than a lot of people will ever be. Life ain't no joke. I'll figure it out and LIVE it somehow before it lives me and I expire. Maybe I think too deeply about things and this is just another rant.

That's where my life is so far....

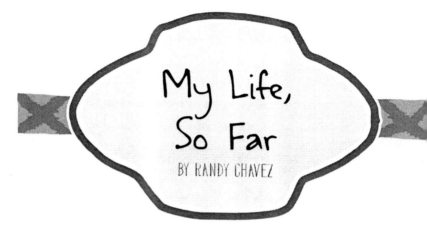

My Life, So Far

BY RANDY CHAVEZ

6 months, already dying

1 year, where's my father?

2 years, Mama, I want milk

3 years, love you, Mom

4 years, "Look, a dog!"

5 years, "You my real dad?"

6 years, "What? The United States?"

7 years, I'm getting bullied

8 years, I want to go back to Mexico

10 years, finally out of elementary school

11 years, lose my grandmother, start drinking

12 years, lose my grandpa and great grandpa

13 years, "This is heavy. Never held a real gun before."

14 years, shoot a gun for the first time

15 years, go on my first drug deal with my uncle

16 years, first time smoking weed

17 years, please be good for me

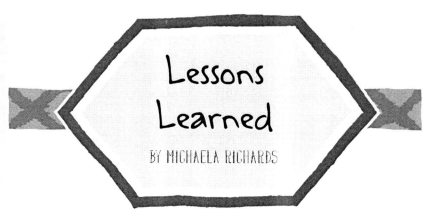

Lessons Learned

BY MICHAELA RICHARDS

My life so far has been a mixture of hate and love
A life full of talking to my father from the heavens above
A life that revolves around my sister and mother
A life that prevents me from ever seeing my brother
In my life I have to worry if my boyfriend is okay
I have to worry about if he makes it home every day
Because before, the Bloods and the Crips were the threat
But now, one look at his skin and even the police want him dead
Lately my life has been full with the words "college degree"
And the anxiety of getting into a university
My life has been full of big sister duties
And protecting my sister because boys no longer have the cooties
In life, my main focus was to not end up like everyone else
Lazy, on my ass, and can't do anything for myself
I don't need to be rich, I need to be secure
So when my mom asks for something I can give it to her for sure
My life has been filled with reconstructing myself
With getting rid of all the sadness that I have felt

In 2009 I had to learn to be strong
I had to come to the realization that my father was gone
I had to realize that people come and go
And realizing that it's natural, you know?
I've learned so far that it's all about your character
When you have only one burger, but you see the homeless
woman and you share with her
My life so far has been filled with lessons learned
And getting through the times when those lessons burned

13 Wishes

BY ZENAIDA JIMENEZ

I feel that my life's plan has been shattered into pieces, completely wiped from my brain.

I wish there was a re-set button I could push that would undo all the mistakes I've made in my personal life and in my education.

I wish I had the courage to have stood up for my younger brother when he was bullied in elementary school.

I wish I had listened as a freshman to my senior friends who told me not to mess up in school. I'm paying for it now.

I wish I didn't see myself as a failure, an idiot, and I wish I could see the things I've accomplished.

I wish I had high self-esteem and could accept myself for the way God created me and see the beauty in his creation.

I wish I had the confidence to achieve my number one goal: To earn an ADN degree in nursing.

I wish I had some sort of talent that I could be proud of. Like being an artist/painter or being a math whiz or excel in a sport. I'd like to be something special, something that isn't common.

I wish my siblings would stop looking at me as if I were still a little girl who can't make her own decisions.

I wish my siblings would stop telling me I won't graduate on time.

I wish my father had preferred his kids over money.

I wish my father had never left for Mexico with a huge amount of money he'd been saving.

I wish he had left some money behind for his kids, rather than being a coward and leaving his children and his mother with nothing.

I wish my life were easier and I had the skills to cope.

I wish.

I wish.

UNDERSTAND US

JAYVON MURRAY
Portrait by Chris Wright

Seven Years Ago

BY BIANCA LOPEZ

My name is Bianca but known as B.

Have you ever felt that feeling that your whole life has changed, and you feel empty inside? When you feel like you're trapped in the middle of the road, crying for help, but no one can hear you? Well, you want to know something? I felt that way only worse—I felt like someone had forced his hands inside me and removed my soul.

I remember this girl who showed people how to smile and laugh even though she had problems behind that pretty face. She knew how to hide her worries, and nobody noticed. People didn't believe there could be anything wrong with her because she was always that smiling, happy girl. But they were wrong. They didn't know her. *I* am her. I am Bianca Lopez.

It was my first year at Mark Twain Middle School. New friends, new teachers, new everything. Just the same life! Oh yeah! Let's not forget new boys! That was the best year, 2008. I had everything I'd ever wanted. Well, not everything, not my brother. But you know what? That was okay because I knew I would see him every eight days and he would be home within three to six months, because boot camp isn't prison.

Months went by and Christmas came around! Now, this was the BEST Christmas ever. I had my family, friends and most of all, my auntie Angela, and my brother, Jordan, was coming home! YAY! I hoped this time it was for good, not just temporary. I knew my auntie was fighting for her life against cancer, but she still looked beautiful as she always had, and she showed me how to be strong and not to be afraid of anything. That day I knew everything would be okay....

I spoke too soon.

January 29, 2009 was the day my whole life changed completely. My beautiful angel passed away. Cancer killed her. A week later, Jordan was taken to jail for something he didn't even do. What had I done to deserve something so horrible? It was a nightmare. I didn't eat, sleep, didn't want to talk to anyone, didn't go to school for almost two weeks and when I did go back, I distanced myself from everyone. I didn't want people to pity me.

When they took my brother away, I blamed him for not being the brother he should have been. I didn't want to write to him or talk to him when he called, and when I did talk to him I just started crying because I forgot everything that had happened. When I was younger I pretended he was traveling around the world and was only able to call when he had time. I was in my denial phase, not believing he was really locked up the way he had been for almost my whole life.

It hurts knowing that your brother has been in boot camps, juvies, and now prison. I wish that at least one year I wasn't receiving wishes for my birthday in letters. I wish for my birthday I had him. All he needed to do was back away from trouble and be a brother and support us!

I know I shouldn't blame him. I know he feels regret all the time. I know he wishes he were here with us. I once told myself that this world had nothing left for me, no reason for me to live, that my life was over. Someone once told me that I have to live life while I'm still young, that I have to keep my head up, live through this and everything will be okay. All I had to do was keep smiling to fool people, to show them nothing was wrong with me. I'd never spoken about where I was from or the struggles I face because I didn't want anyone to feel sorry for me. I didn't want anyone to judge me.

Now it's 2016, and that girl of seven years ago is gone. Now she is proud, independent, confident, strong, smart, a new Bianca. Thanks to POPS. I'm not afraid or too shy to speak about my life. I don't care what others say. I love my brother with all my heart, and I'm glad my auntie is gone because she's in a better place. If it wasn't for Amy, Danziger, my auntie, Jordan, my parents and POPS, I wouldn't be where I am now.

I FOUND MYSELF AND I'M HOME.

I Don't Need Help

BY MADISON ABERCROMBIE

I lie on the floor. I try to find a way to move, to power my own body. Without anyone else's help.

I fit my brace over my right knee and try to stand. I grab onto the first thing my hand touches, my bedpost.

I realize that nothing can help me.

I try to use my arms to push off the ground and lift myself up. But I lack the strength to lift my 102-pound body.

"You've got this, Maddy," I say to myself. "Just a few steps to go to the bathroom. C'mon, Maddy. A one-year-old can do this. You've got this."

But I don't.

I never imagined walking to the bathroom would be a struggle. Well, maybe when I'm old and need a "Life-Alert" necklace, but not at 15. Not when if I'm not walking or running everywhere, I'm skateboarding everywhere.

It's 4 a.m.

I've spent the past 90 minutes trying to stand on my own.

At 5:30, I give up.

I hate the way people stare at me when I walk. The same look they give homeless people; the look *I* give homeless people. The look one gives a homeless person when we want to offer help, but we can't or we don't.

I hate the look that says, "What happened to you?" "Why can't you walk?"

"I can do it!" I yell at my sister Jasmine who wants to help me dress.

"Maddy, please. It's no big deal. Let me help," she says.

I blow her off and try to balance on my good leg.

"Maddy, please."

I lean against the wall trying to balance while pulling on my shirt.

"I can do it!" I insist.

My body aches as I slip on my shirt.

My road burn on my lower back bleeds, but I keep quiet. Else Jasmine will make me change my shirt, and I can't go through that again.

"Madison," my mother calls. "Are you dressed yet?"

Then she's standing in the doorway, and I lose my balance. I fall. My leg bangs against my bed. My mom rushes over, but I refuse her help.

"I can do it, Mommy. I'm not three years old. I can dress myself. Please, just let me do it."

As I speak she sits on the floor beside me, helping me change.

I can't skateboard to the corner store for an Arizona iced tea. I can't go to school. I'm going to miss the last three weeks of the fall semester and what happens to my grades? My credits? Only one teacher has checked in. The administration has said nothing. Perhaps a kid getting hit by a car is not an extraordinary event.

Yet another doctor's appointment. I fear he will say that I am as broken as I feel.

"You might have a hairline fracture," he says.

And what does that mean?

"Keep your brace on and do not walk without your crutches."

Early January.

Another week until spring semester begins.

I feel like a robot. I walk but without bending my knees.

My sisters, Jasmine and Danny, are about to walk to the store.

"I'm coming," I yell.

They sit and wait patiently for me.

I attempt to walk "normal."

I trip and fall down the stairs. I crawl to the kitchen.

"Baby!" my mom screams. "Baby!"

My mom's fiancé falls to his knees, slowly picks me up and places me back onto my bed. My knee shakes uncontrollably. I try to hold it down, but it seems as if it has a life of its own and wobbles every which way.

I try not to cry. But I fail, and breathing is next to impossible.

My mom holds me, "Breathe Maddy, breathe."

She strokes my hair. I am a child again.

Unwelcome thoughts rush through my mind, "I can't do it. I can't walk. I can't run." My mind reels backward to the moment of impact. I step off the curb and Wham!

I am being rushed to a hospital.

I remember my father crying as he stared at me while I lay in a hospital bed, my eyes barely cracked, my back bleeding, my neck in a brace, my leg swollen to the size of a watermelon.

I remember the ambulance ride. My mother holds my hand, gripping it tightly. I remember the moment of my sudden immobilization. The bus bench eight inches away, and I couldn't make my way off the asphalt to safety. I remember screaming from pain, the sounds coming as if from someone else's newly wracked body. I remember that next morning. The day I realized I would need help. The day I realized my leg would never be the same. That I would always walk with a slight limp.

I try my hardest to appear normal.

I try not to replay that moment when I tumbled over the hood of the car and flew in the air and landed on Venice Boulevard and lost consciousness for a few minutes.

As my mom strokes my hair I don't bother to refuse her help. I don't ask her to leave me alone so I can calm myself. I look at her and I accept her love, her sweet, motherly embrace, and I feel, for the moment, that I "just can't do it alone."

Warrior

BY KHYRA BLACK

So I'm a Christian. I've accepted Jesus Christ as my savior. Which is great, I know. Trust me I know. But being a Christian my whole life, I know what it takes. And trust me. It's not filled with sugar cookies, sunshine and rainbows. Jesus even pointed out to me in his word that it would be hard. That life is hard.

Jesus knew that life is hard (they tried to throw Him off a cliff, they mocked Him, and they eventually crucified Him), and He told us that just being in this world we would have trouble and tribulation (John 16:33). But now where do I stand?

There is no list of rules about how a Christian teen should act. But there is common sense and there are the Ten Commandments, the basics... "Thou shalt not kill." "Thou shalt not commit adultery." "Honor thy mother and father..." and seven more. But how do I do just that?

How do I, as a teen who gets peer pressured every day not steal, not talk back to my parents, not have thoughts about wanting to have sex and not waiting until I'm married? How do I not get made fun of for waiting until I'm married?

It's too much! The pressure, that is. Inside I kick and scream! And I yell in my mind: Why is it so hard for me? For a Christian?

I fall into the trap. I do things I know I'm not supposed to do. I would be ashamed to tell my mother or grandmother what I've done because I know how a young Christian girl is supposed to act.

So I cry. I cry and cry and cry for help from God. For answers. For a way out.

And then I pray: Why me? Why can't I be the perfect young Christian girl you want me to be? Why is it so hard? I love you so much. And I want to be close to you. I want to make it to heaven. I don't want to be left behind. So why do I continue to hurt you?

Then it clicks. God never said it would be easy. He never handed me a perfect life. I have to fight. Every day. A spiritual battle. Warfare. For my God. I have to try. It's not going to be easy. I'm going to make mistakes. I'm going to fall down but I have to get up. I have to realize I chose God to be part of my life. And He made me. He loved me enough to die for me. And I love Him enough to make Him happy.

So I get up, I wipe my tears, and I carry on. With my day. With my life. Being a Warrior. And letting God fight my battles for me, striving every day to be a great Christian.

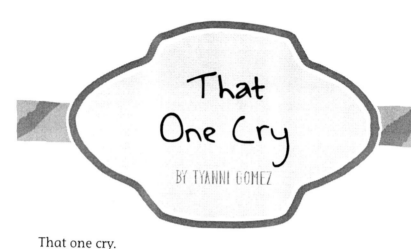

That One Cry

BY TYANNI GOMEZ

That one cry.
You lock that door behind you.
You put your bag down.
You slouch and you are just tired.
You take off that smile and your eyes
They are just so tired and numb.
You walk back and forth.
You talk to yourself. "Just breathe."
You try to calm yourself and breathe heavily.
You stand and keep controlling that breathing.
You start to tap your feet on the wooden floors.
You're biting your nails for the nerves that bothered you
And there you go, you replay everything in your head.

Then it breaks.

You have that one tear fall down from your brown eyes.
Your hands move through your hair and drop roughly.
You look at your books, photos of you smiling, papers.
You smack every little thing to the floor and stand.
You turn and see your bed.

You crawl on and lie down on your bed.

You crumple yourself up.
And you just cry.
In a matter of seconds your lips are shaking.
Your eyes sting so badly, you have to wipe them.
You have your arms around your waist because it hurts.
You feel like you can't get enough air through those tears.
Then, you cry in such silence, you cover your mouth.
You cough a bit, just a little, just so you won't choke.

It's a bad cry when you know this hurts so bad that you want
to stop the pain.

And you stop. Your tears are still falling across your beautiful
face.
Your make-up is ruined. You just lie there and stare towards
the wall in front of you.
And once she cared so much, she got up, wiped off the tears...
She didn't care one bit, not even at all.

All because of that one cry.

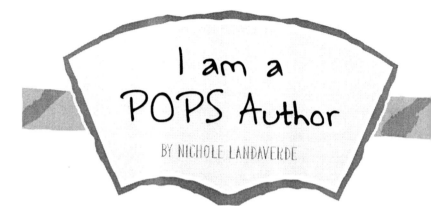

I am a POPS Author

BY NICHOLE LANDAVERDE

I am a POPS author
I hear many moving stories from those in our club
I see tears form as these authors read their stories
I want to portray the same understanding I have of them to others through my writing

I am a POPS author

I pretend to be shy because I'd rather listen than speak
I feel the pain it brings them to read aloud
I worry that their words will overpower them
I cry from empathy when I hear their voices crack
I understand what they want to portray

I am a POPS author

Theme from English B*

BY ANONYMOUS

The instructor said,

Go home and write
a page tonight
And let that page come out of you
Then it'll be true.

I am a shy girl
I wonder if I will ever become outgoing
But I don't want to be outgoing sometimes
I enjoy my own quiet atmosphere

I wonder if the people around me can relate to me
I wonder what people think of me
Do they like me?
I don't think so; otherwise they would talk to me.

I have a voice, but I'd rather not use it
I'm just too shy to speak first
So I sit alone
Feeling like I have no one

Because most of the time I don't have anyone
I think, "Do I ever fit in?"
That's when I realize I don't fit, but that's okay.
There's only one person I can trust

Myself, because I'd never hurt myself
Besides, it's okay to be different, sometimes
Everyone's different
And being different is normal

At least I hope it is
Eventually people will like me
So there's no need to worry or care
Hopefully, I can be myself someday, somewhere

*Based on a poem by Langston Hughes

THE UNKNOWN WRITER
Portrait by Chris Wright

Enervate

BY HEAVEN VIDAÑA

You see me.
You hear me.
I seem strong.

I say I'll fight hard.
I'll show him wrong.

I work hard.
I try to stay strong.

But you're right.
Inside I am weak.
Inside I am holding
Millions of tears.

When you bring him up,
It feels as if I'm
Losing the strings
That hold me together.

Most people think I'm lucky
because "he's still in the
picture," but he's not.

He's gone.

No one understands my pain.
No one knows how empty
My heart feels.
Just like I don't
Know what they feel.

They can't claim or judge what's inside of me.

My life will always be filled
With this painful curiosity.

But I have to stay strong and
Show him wrong.

Still, I Feel Blessed

BY ANONYMOUS

Student, neighbor, child,
but always labeled "illegal immigrant."

Wondering how I will be successful when growing up I thought I was a criminal,
a criminal trying to grasp English words my teachers spoke during the day and teaching those words to my mom at night.

"Illegal immigrants," is what we children who are full of dreams are called.
We, who dream of being, lawyers, doctors and police
Who want to make our communities better.

We're more than illegal immigrants; we are children who do not want to inherit the jobs our parents have to do.

Sometimes I feel dehumanized knowing that one day I could turn from student to criminal.

Still, I feel blessed
To be in a country with some opportunities.

THE BOARD SPEAKS

I AM

BY CHAIM DUNBAR

I am black. Like the middle of the darkest mid summer's night out there in the back woods of the Deep South where runaway slaves would use the hues of their African skin trying to blend in with shadows, filled with fear fleeing for freedom in search of Miss Tubman's Underground

Black, like soul food and corn rolls, ebony keys on a piano and faces too seldom seen on prime time TV shows. I am black.

Just slightly darker than my mother. A beautiful sista from Manhattan's Lower East Side who survived the nineteen fifties and sixties when the word nigger rolled off the tongues of whites as though it were the national anthem but I am black.

Descendant of a people who are the architects of civilization, astronomers & mathematicians that were kings and rulers long before the Greeks, Romans or Dr. Martin Luther Jr. The original man I am whose legacies have been erased from the pages of American history and replaced by his-story?

I am black, full of big dreams wide awake in an inner city nightmare. The usual suspect with thick lips, kinky hair and no need for SPF. Because of me, there is jazz and R&B, Rock

& Roll, Hip Hop, Soul, open heart surgery, automatic elevator doors, peanuts and magnum sized condoms.

Forced to compete on an uneven playing field, fighting an uphill battle, facing 100 mile per hour winds and still I stand. Here and now. Healing the scars of my past so that I can exist in the present and make it to the future with enough courage and self-esteem to not be ashamed of who I am.

I AM BLACK and I LOVE ME!

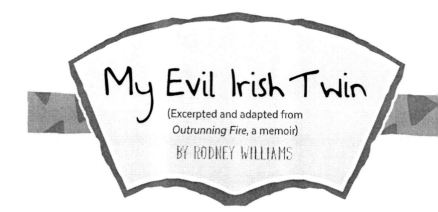

My Evil Irish Twin

(Excerpted and adapted from
Outrunning Fire, a memoir)

BY RODNEY WILLIAMS

I got the call from my sister, Lisa, at 2 a.m. "Randy burned the house down."

∽

I was born nine months after my brother, Randy—Irish twins.

My earliest memories involve our dressing like twins, doing dance routines for company. He taught me math and common sense. He was funny and worldly, able to talk his way in or out of any situation. He taught me how to evade the police by dipping off into the hilly red clay between houses on the motorcycles our father bought us.

I learned early to conform, to be obedient, to disappear. Randy learned the opposite. We stopped dressing alike. The older we got, the more different we became. I was the nerdy, scrawny loner, he the charming, athletic socialite.

∽

Randy first went to prison when he was fifteen. For a while, every Saturday morning our family piled into the car to drive two hours to see him, until one day when I was sixteen I decided I wasn't going anymore. I didn't like the long

316

waits, the searches, the rules about what we couldn't have on our possession, constantly being watched by guards. I hated barbed wire and watch towers and uniforms. My mother tried to shame me for not going, but I didn't care. Academic and musical awards I won in high school went largely unnoticed. They were unable to soothe the heartache of losing a first son to prison.

Randy came home from prison when he was eighteen. After my father died he started stealing and threatening my mother. She slept with her purse and feared for her life. By then I lived far away, working to create a life so pure it would counter the depravity of my brother's.

⁓

Lisa wasn't at Sunday dinner the day Randy burned the house down, but she told me the story that ended with Randy filling a gas can from the pump, dousing the house, fixing a plate of leftovers from Sunday dinner, leisurely eating, striking a match, and walking out.

Over the years, as I lived in different cities, that house was what I meant when I said "home." My baby pictures, the afghan my grandmother made for me when I was born, my school trophies, burned up in that house.

That Monday morning at 2 a.m., Randy ceased being my enemy. He ceased to exist.

Eleven years later, I was arrested for paying a business tax late during the recession. As an indifferent corrections officer led me down a depressing corridor, for the first time I wondered if Randy had ever been able to recover from prison, years of not being trusted, treated without dignity. I wondered if anyone could. Listening to the recorded voice announcing

a collect call from me—"an inmate at a correctional facility," I flashed backed to those time- and money-sucking calls that came regularly during my teenage years. I stood uncomfortably in a tiny cell waiting for the call to connect, and I understood why my brother had desperately needed those calls.

Until that day, I never felt called to do anything about our nation's habit of incarcerating people--particularly young men of color. Like most people, I decided the solution to the problem of astronomical incarceration rates, the marginalization and mistreatment of people on the wrong end of the criminal justice system, was to make sure I never got incarcerated.

Had I bothered to think long enough about it, I would have recognized that in America it becomes harder every day to make sure one never goes to jail.

Randy died early in the morning, sitting in a chair. He'd refused to go to bed the night before, perhaps thinking if he didn't close his eyes, death couldn't take him.

At the funeral I sat dead center of the first pew, looking into his open casket and his lifeless face three feet away. Friends spoke fondly about how incorrigible he was, how hard-headed. In the same breath, they spoke of his loyalty, his sense of humor, his philosophical musings. They spoke of my brother's flaws and virtues with equal fondness. I realized then that I'd never given him the gift of understanding and of nuance, and that I'd never accepted that gift for myself.

As the preacher flailed his robed arms I realized that in society's eyes, my brother and I were the same: dangerous Black men trying to outrun the same fire—the fire we'd been born into. We used different tactics. Neither of us had succeeded.

Until that moment I'd neglected to understand how easily I might have been the one lying in that casket, if only the gasoline of mental illness, drug addiction, and incarceration at age fifteen had been poured on my fire.

I looked into my brother's face and made a promise:

I will not disappear.

I will be who I authentically am.

I will fight to stop this pain.

Even if it burns the house down.

RODNEY WILLIAMS
Portrait by Chris Wright

319

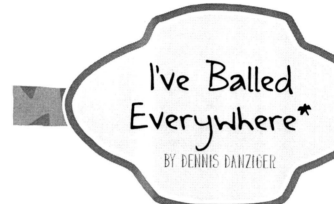

I've Balled Everywhere*

BY DENNIS DANZIGER

I was shooting hoops at Moore Park, watching my 3-pointers
drop, when this shirtless, tattooed brutha quipped,
"You musta had some game back in the day, Pop."
I ignored this poser for as long as I could stand.
Then I looked him in the eye and said, "I've balled everywhere,
man. I've balled everywhere."

I balled in Westwood, Brentwood and Hollywood,
I balled in suburbs, and in the 'hood, where I was pretty damn
good.
I balled in Boston, Austin, Houston, River Oaks,
That's where George W. Bush grew up, what a joke.
I balled in daylight and in the dark,
Balled in Mar Vista and Central Park.

I balled everywhere man,
I balled everywhere.

I balled in Converse All-Stars that we called Chucks,
balled against hustlers who took my twenty bucks.
I balled in Jordans, Nikes and PF Flyers,
but none of them kicks could make this boy jump any higher.

I balled everywhere man,
I balled everywhere.

I balled wired on coffee, and once I balled high on weed,
yet none of that stuff affected my speed.
Had White Man's Disease since I was a kid
couldn't get off the ground, whatever substance I did.

I balled with short hair and when I let my hair go,
I balled in college with a six-inch Afro.
I balled against Jimmy Blacklock who coaches the Harlem
Globetrotters,
and once on the court I was mistaken for that dude from "Wel-
come Back, Kotter."

I balled everywhere man,
I balled everywhere.

I played Horses against teachers from Venice and Samohi,
learned that when it comes to the score, some teachers will lie.
I balled on church courts and on New York City streets,
where you can go up for a rebound and come down dead meat
I balled against Kobi in the Palihi gym,
He dunked on me twice; I couldn't touch the rim.

I balled three years at Bellaire High,
so many memories are indelible,
like when my redneck coach said,
"Danziger, for a white boy you're good,
for a Jew, you're incredible."
I balled everywhere man,
I balled everywhere.

*Inspired by Jeff Mack's *I've Been Everywhere*, made famous by Johnny Cash.

Advice to Ninth Graders

You're not going to end the year with the
same people you started with.
~*Jamayca Dearborn*

I wish someone would have told me that they care about my
education. I wish someone told me that once you graduate
you'll lose contact with most of your friends.
~*Bianca Lopez*

Don't spend your time wishing for the ideal high school
experience, enjoy the experience you're having.
~*Ryan Silver, Culver City High School*

Don't fall for the jerks.
~*Mariana Hernandez*

Go to class every day and you'll be cooler
than the cool kids...after graduation.
~*D. Jones*

Bring your own lunch and snacks.
~*Anonymous*

Don't smoke weed in the restrooms...they may lock the doors.
~*Anonymous*

ANGEL DE LA CRUZ
Portrait by Doris Longman

Author Bios

Madson Abercrombie is a family-oriented girl who is trying to figure out who she is and she moves closer to finding that out every time she writes. Her essays have appeared online on *The Good Men Project* and *Narratively*. Madison's essay won third place in the 2016 Beverly Hills Literary Society Awards.

Haley Alvarez. I am a student from RFK LAHSA (Los Angeles High School of the Arts) who enjoys cats, painting, and writing about life experiences whether they're good or not so good.

Mireya Sanchez Annibali Peace, love, positivity.

Vanessa Barajas is an 18-year-old who loves writing, watching movies and developing skills for art.

John Bembry, a young ambitious African American bringing peace though the pain he embraces. With music, with words, and creativity.

Khyra Black is a senior, a Christian, a teenager who speaks her mind.

Brian Campos is an 18-year-old who dreams of records to break, who listens for silence to herald peace, and who hopes for his love to be received.

Michelle Cardoza is a 16-year-old girl who is in love with dogs.

Randy Chavez is a senior at Venice High who likes to party even though he looks like a nerd. He plans to attend West LA College to make his parents happy.

Anthony Cortez was a lost soul who found a path to a better world with guidance and a pencil.

Tania Cruz is striving to meet her goals to graduate and succeed in life to make her parents happy.

Jessica De La Mora. I'm a 16-year-old who was having problems, and then I found POPS.

Valeria DeLa Torre has big dreams.

Luis Fajardo has been published in the past two POPS the Club anthologies and will continue to write after he graduates from high school in June 2016.

Maynor Galletan. A just-legal adult who's been acting like one for a long time.

Lilliana Garcia. A 15-year-old girl, wishing she can get her father-daughter relationship back.

Maria Garcia is a sophomore at Venice High with dreams and goals she hopes to achieve one day.

Tyanni Gomez. An 18-year-old teenager chasing her dream to be part of the law enforcement, but her passion for writing will remain in her heart.

Yesenia Gomez. I am a 16-year-old survivor and my scars can prove it.

Daniel Gonzalez. A 17-year-old boy, supported mostly by his mother, and who is graduating high school this year, to attend Cal State Northridge.

Emiria Henry is a 16-year-old junior at Lawndale High School, and she always shows her love, respect, and acceptance for others. She wants everyone to feel like they have a voice of their own through her writings.

Angela Hernandez a joyful 18-year-old who loves sharing her stories. She's the youngest in her family and loves spending time with them.

Juanito Hernandez. Dark past, looking to make a bright future for himself. Full of pride yet looking for the definition of humble. Till then, his personality is like Yeezus with a bit of Jesus.

Mariana Hernandez Writing will ease the mind. POPS the Club is the way to go, the way to my home.

Miranda Hughes likes history, writing, and '90s R&B.

Zenaida Jimenez is a Venice High 12th grader who is ready to move on to college where she plans to earn her ADN and RN degrees in nursing.

D. Jones #2 19 years young, with an imagination; making my odds even.

Nichole Landaverde will put herself in your shoes.

Bianca Lopez known as B, is a Venice Graduate Class of 2015! I show this world my huge smile and I eat plenty of food.

Daisy Lopez known as DaisyDukes living life to the fullest with hope and pride.

Leslie Mateos is a 2015 Venice High graduate who loves to return to visit POPS the Club.

Kei-Arri McGruder is a 17-year-old African American student at Venice High School.

Desireé "Desi" Miller will be moving to Arizona after graduation from Venice High in 2015 and will attend a community college in Arizona.

Luis Nunez is a 2015 graduate of Venice High School and a graphic designer.

Paradyse Oakley is a junior at Lawndale High School who loves to express and expand her horizon aspiration is to become a Criminal Justice Lawyer or Politician.

Glorious Lanette Owens is an 18-year-old girl trying to make sure she never has to worry about money for education ever again. Glorious's essay took first prize in the 2016 Beverly Hills Literary Society Awards.

Jose Pina lives life as if it's his last day. He grew up in the surf/skate culture and appreciates his community, his home, Venice, CA.

Elsa Ramirez is a 17-year-old girl with big dreams of becoming successful.

Jameka Reynolds graduated from Venice High School in early 2016.

Michaela Richards graduated from Venice High School in 2015.

Jesse Rodriguez Death may be miles away, but live in the present. Your destination is also miles away.

Jocelin Ruano grew up in and has lived in South Central L.A. all her life. She's 18 with lots of ambition to pursue her dreams.

Rosa Isela Ruiz is a really happy girl from the outside who suffers from the inside.

Rosa Maria Ruiz is a 17-year-old girl, graduating from Venice High this year, chasing my dreams to become an actress.

Rosio Salas is 17 and a junior at Venice High, hoping for the best.

Iona Scott is a 17-year-old senior at Venice High who writes the truth that others can relate to.

Katherine Secaida is a junior in high school who fears her dark past, but expresses it through writing.

Kobe Tomas Sometimes you got to be uncomfortable in life.

Dianne Vasquez is an 18-year-old girl who is going to be in the real world in less than three months but feels more alive than ever.

Heaven Vidaña is a student from RFK LAHSA (LA High School of the Arts) who prefers speaking through paper and pen than communicating with people.

Mona Viera is 17 and was born on New Years, New Year, New me.

Colbie Witherspoon is a 17-year-old senior planning to attend San Francisco State University with a BS in Business Administration Management.

Ivori Wyche is a 15-year-old girl, ready to be greater than her past.

Friends of POPS Bios

Calvin Collier is a writer at California Medicla Facility, Vacaville, California and supporter of POPS the Club.

Dennis Danziger teaches English at Venice HS and regularly defeats his students in 3-point shooting contests. He is also the co-founder of POPS the Club and sponsor of the Venice High chapter.

Michael Davis is a writer and co-founder of the Writers' Guild at California Medical Facility, Vacaville, California

Papa Bear De La Mora wishes to thank POPS the Club for all they do for my beloved daughter, Jessica.

Chaim Dunbar is a performer, writer and member of the Board of Directors of POPS the Club.

Alison Longman, co-editor of this volume, is a 26-year-old who's still trying to figure it all out.

Doris Longman studied art at UCLA and is a new friend of POPS the Club.

John Rodriguez is a born writer and a recent college graduate, currently serving time at Ironwood State Prison.

Rodney Williams is an author, an innkeeper and a member of the Board of Directors of POPS the Club

Chris Wright teaches art at Venice High School and in his spare time hikes, surfs, reads, and sits in trees. His sketches in this volume were done during POPS the Club meetings.

Boston Woodard was a POPS kid before there was a POPS the Club.

PORTRAITS: John Bembry & Angel De La Cruz graduated from Venice High in 2015 and are currently attending college; Randy Chavez, Linda Duran, Tyanni Gomez, Juanito Hernandez, Miranda Hughes, Kei-Arri McGruder, Jayvon Murray, Glorious Owens, Rosa Isela Ruiz, Rosa Maria Ruiz & Katherine Secaida are students at Venice High and members of Venice POPS.

SUNSET PHOTOGRAPH
Photograph by Juanito Hernandez

Acknowledgements

Thank you to all the members of POPS Lumberjack High in Bemidji, Minnesota and to sponsor, Rebecca Rittenour, for the title of this year's anthology.

POPS the Club would not be possible without the dedication of our remarkable club sponsors: Dennis Danziger (Venice High), Sharyl Larson (Conley-Caraballo High), Michelle Lee (Lawndale High), Andrès Reconco (Los Angeles High School of the Arts), Rebecca Rittenour (Lumberjack High), Stephanie Sauter (LA High). In addition to opening their doors and their hearts to the students of POPS the Club, Sharyl and Rebecca cook, shop and otherwise make certain there's always lunch.

At POPS the Club, our motto and the way we begin each meeting is:

First We Eat

For not only do the meals we share create community, they nourish and inspire our memories, intellects and imaginations.

We wish to thank those who make these meals possible: Debbie Ullman and everyone at Factors Famous Deli in Los Angeles; Steve Cohen at Village Pizzeria in Larchmont Village; Kristin Robbins at Manhattan Bread & Bagel in Manhattan Beach; Fernando, Elizabeth and Bricia Lopez at Guelaguetza Restaurante in Los Angeles; everyone at Le Pain Quotidien, Marina Del Rey, California; Tory Toyama and everyone at Panera Bread in Marina Del Rey.

We are looking forward to welcoming clubs from Seattle, Washington, Midland/Odessa, Texas, Toledo, Ohio, Akron, Ohio, and other parts of California in the coming months. Thank you Laura Rocker, Debra Sheldon, Callie Gregory, Anna-Majia Lee, Judi Ashley Murphy, Alice Quinn, Diana Fox-Gallagher, Virgie Hamrick, Emily Numbers, Robert Barton, Jana Boccalon and Karie DeLarme for helping us to bring POPS the Club to high schools everywhere.

Our brilliant staff make everything possible. Thank you Mel Keedle, Program Manager; Lauren Marks, Social Media Director; and Arrowyn Ambrose, Volunteer Coordinator.

Without our volunteers, this volume and our weekly meetings would not be possible. Thank you:

Stacey Cohan, Margot Dougherty, Sarah Ellenberg, Carl Finer, Jessica Gutierrez, Mark Hoadley, Jenna Hughes, Angel Jennings, Christina Larsen, Alison Longman, Bianca Lopez, Natalie Lima, Christina McDowell, Katharine Nyhus, Gary Phillips, Laurenne Sala, Kelly Slattery, Teagan Smith, Madge Stein Woods, Enrique Solis, Tory Toyama, Hazel Kight Witham, and Chris Wright.

Thank you to our webmaster extraordinaire, John Ciccolini; to our brilliant design team, Kenny Barela & Molly Danziger Johnson; to Ivaylo Getov, filmmaker; to Jessica Tuck of Spark Off Rose; to Tim Allen and Jamie Masada of the Laugh Factory for your generosity; to dedicated mentor Rachel Davenport for your wisdom, to David Factor, Vicky Foxworth, and Janet McIntyre at Executive Services Corps Los Angeles for your guidance and support; to fellow Executive Directors and spirit guides: Scott Budnick, Tim Carpenter, Amy Fass, Michele Neff Hernandez, Bill Thompson, and Kelley Whitis; to Gabriella Goldberg and Kate Savage of Brentwood School for your artistry; to Doris Longman for your exquisite portraits; to Christina Larsen for your keen eyes and large heart; to Amanda Keller Konya for your photographic genius; to our brilliant teaching artists Antonio Sacre, Susan Treadwell and Alicia Sedwick.

Thank you to Gwen Jones and Caryn Bruno at Barnes & Noble at The Grove, Los Angeles and to Eric Sims and the staff at the Kirk Douglas Theatre in Culver City, California for providing the stages on which our students' work is invited to shine.

Thank you to the men of the Writers' Guild at California Medical Facility State Prison, Vacaville for your continuing financial and emotional support.

Thank you to Amy Cheney & the librarians of *In the Margins Award* for recognizing and celebrating our authors' beautiful work in our two previous anthologies, *Runaway Thoughts & Ghetto By the Sea*.

Thank you to *The Good Men Project* and editor Wilhelm Cortez for publishing our students' work each week; and to the editors at *Narrative.ly* for recognizing the importance of our students' stories and sharing them with the world.

Thank you to the Anderson Foundation, to Berkshire Hathaway, to the Jewish Federation of Los Angeles Change-makers Award & to Alicia Estrada Castro and The California Endowment for your generous support.

Thank you to the Venice High School Alumni Association for your grant as part of your Excellence in Education Program that helped to support this volume.

Thank you to our angel, Madge Stein Woods.

Oceans of gratitude to our Board of Directors who guide us every step of the way: Lydia Flora Barlow, Carol F. Burton, Dennis Danziger, Chaim Dunbar, Anastasia Stanecki, Heidi Tuffias, & Rodney Williams.

Language exerts hidden power,
like the moon on the tides.

RITA MAE BROWN